The Organization Woman

Building a Career—
An Inside Report

The Organization Woman

Building a Career—
An Inside Report

Edith L. Highman

Surveys By Arthur Highman, Ph.D.

 HUMAN SCIENCES PRESS,INC.
72 FIFTH AVENUE,
NEW YORK, N.Y. 10011

To Arthur, Mark, Louis, Bruce, and Phyllis

Published by Human Sciences Press, Inc.
72 Fifth Avenue, New York, New York 10011

Printed in the United States of America
987654321

Library of Congress Cataloging in Publication Data

Highman, Edith L.
   The organization woman—building a career.

   Bibliography: p.199
   Includes index.
   1. Women supervisors. 2. Women executives.
I. Highman, Arthur. II. Title
HD6054.3.H54 1985   658.4 '09 '024042   84-27775
ISBN 0-89885-237-4

Contents

List of Tables   7
Foreword   9
Preface   11
1. INTRODUCTION   15
2. FACTORS IN BUILDING A CAREER—PERSONAL
   QUALITIES   20
   Being a Hard Worker   20
   Professional Attitude   22
   Decisiveness   28
   Being Organized   30
   Practicality   31
   Other Assets   34
3. MANAGERIAL TRAITS   35
   Aggressiveness   35
   Articulating   44
   Motivating   45
   Risk-taking   45
   Delegating   47
   Politics   48
4. DEALING WITH PEERS, BOSSES, AND SPOUSES   54
   Competition   54
   "Affirmative Action"   57
   Spouse Pressure   58
   Women on Women   59
   Male Chauvinism   60
   Pay and Promotion   64
   Further Aspects   65
5. DEALING WITH SUBORDINATES   70
   Woman Boss and Male Subordinate   70

Women and Women Bosses		71
Styles of Management		73
Delegating		78
6. OPPORTUNITIES—MAKING THEM, SPOTTING THEM, SEIZING THEM		81
Readiness		81
Where the Opportunities Lie		83
Bosses and Mentors		86
Further Strategies		88
7. CUTTING YOUR LOSSES		91
Reasons to Change Jobs		91
Timing		93
8. UNDERSTANDING YOUR BOSS		96
First Priorities		96
Assessing the Risk Factor		99
9. UNDERSTANDING THE ORGANIZATION		105
When Things Are not what They Seem		105
MBO and the Career Woman		107
Budgets and Forecasts		109
10. CAREER AND MARRIAGE		113
Behind the Demographics		113
Why Wives Work		114
Help or Hindrance?		115
Home, Health, Children		118
11. SEX, SEXUAL OVERTONES, AND PERSONAL PROBLEMS		127
"They Look Instead of Listen"		128
Using Sex		129
Harassment		131
"Getting Involved"		133
Going Places		137
Impermanence		139
12. YOUR LEGAL RIGHTS		141
How Title VII Works		141
Other Legislation		145
The EEOC and Sexual Harassment		146
Further Employee Protection		148
Appendix		150
References		197
Bibliography		199
Index		201

List of Tables
(in Appendix)

Table		Page No.
1.	Profile of Survey Respondents	166
2.	Male Respondents' Perceptions of Organization Women: General Characteristics	168
3.	Male Respondents' Perceptions of Organization Women: Relationships with Subordinates	170
4.	Permanence of a Woman's Employment	171
5.	The Jobs Held by the Organization Women Surveyed	172
6.	Where in the Company the Better-Paid Jobs for Women Are Found	173
7.	How Jobs Are Obtained	174
8.	Reasons for Promotion, Other Than Ability and Performance	176
9.	Job Turnover	177
10.	Stress	178
11.	Job Problems Faced by Women	179
12.	Resentment Faced by Women	183
13.	Discrimination Faced by Women	185
14.	The Married Woman and Her Career	186
15.	Sex and Sexual Overtones—Advantage or Not?	188
16.	Sex and Sexual Overtones—Frequency	190
17.	Use of Sexual Connotation or Sex on the Job by Career Women	192
18.	Factors for Getting Ahead	193
19.	Obstacles to Getting Ahead	194
20.	Men's Difficulties Working with Women	195
21.	Women's Difficulties Working with Men and Women	196

Foreword

*T*here has clearly been considerable progress for women in the past ten years in the business world, as has been much discussed and publicized in various articles, books, newspapers and business journals, and on TV and radio. At the same time, it is apparent that women have not yet achieved total success and equality. Women are still not paid as much as men and certainly are not yet as evident in the top management hierarchy of corporate America. Ultimately, success for women will come when they create their own individual responses to the work situations they meet—responses not predicated solely on being women or on what any one book says, but predicated on being their own unique selves, with individual goals, strengths and strategies.

This book fills an important and hopefully temporary need for women entering the business world and for those interested in further advancement—to learn how others have done it. You may not agree with all of them, and you may not want to approach certain issues in the same way, but reading their stories and advice helps in developing your own approach to success. Because women working in organizations do not yet have enough role models from direct personal observation, it can be most useful to get the benefit of a wide range of experiences and perceptions by reading a book based on survey material gathered from a large number of female and male executives.

The book is not just a compilation of survey opinions and statistical summaries, and it is not a simplistic "here's the formula to success" book. In key critical areas it provides sound practical advice on how to resolve problems—or indicates how others have—and points to some actions to take or avoid. Frequently there is no perfect or universal solution for the problems women face in today's business world. Part of the value of this book lies in informing women about the possible courses of action and educating them as to the ramifications of each. At some level the book provides information important for any business manager who wants to be politically astute and savvy about the business game. What it says about management and organizational behavior is relevant to men as well as women. As a collection of other people's experiences, perceptions and opinions, this book proceeds on several levels and deals effectively with many issues that women face today as they seek to build their own unique approach to successful careers in American business organizations.

Sofia Galson
Senior Vice President and
Chief Financial Officer
The Pacific Stock Exchange, Inc.
San Francisco, CA

Preface

This book is about the factors, personal and managerial, which affect the organization woman in building her career. It differs from other books about career women because it combines the results of extensive national surveys of both female and male executives and managers of large corporations with experience and observations over many years on how the people who run U.S. business and industry operate. The confidential surveys, and subsequent personal interviews conducted in 1982–1984, provide perceptions of top male bosses about career women who work with and for them; and also perceptions about what the organization women think about themselves, their careers, and their male peers and bosses. These perceptions are extensively expressed in their own words.

The wide-ranging surveys undertaken provide opinions and information on factors, other than job performance alone, that the organization woman needs to consider in pursuing her career. A significant aspect of these studies is that the respondents were men and women from all parts of the country working in a great variety of fields—heavy industry to high technology—and not limited only to those in public relations or advertising, or in banking, retailing, or cosmetics, where so many of the traditionally publicized top career women in business organizations are found.

11

The surveys and interviews completed provide important insights into factors which can affect progress in a woman's career. The findings include some surprises such as the presence of more male bias, female fears and career/marriage complications than might have been thought. This book discusses the personal and managerial characteristics of organization women and compares them with their male counterparts; factors important in getting ahead; what the problems are in working with men and with other women; the impact of male chauvinism; where and how the better jobs are to be found; how promotions have been obtained; the working environment, including sexual overtones; and the interrelationships of marriage, family, career, health, and the quality of life.

Chapters that may prove of special interest to women building their careers are those on *Understanding Your Boss* and *Understanding the Organization.* To the woman who would climb the corporate ladder such understanding is crucial. A chapter on women's legal rights in employment is also included.

There has been a lot written about women with dazzling careers—and more power to them. But here is a book designed for the many women now employed, or considering employment in business and industry, going for long-haul success with steady progression, real and continuing challenge, satisfactions, and monetary rewards. It is also intended for male executives and managers who work with women and who may wish better to understand the problems and viewpoints of career women. A greater understanding of how men and women feel about each other and themselves in the work place can only be helpful in furthering more harmonious work relationships between the sexes.

Since every woman is unique, each one will of course apply in her own way what she will have learned from this book, for

To each one is given a marble to carve for the wall;
A stone that is needed to heighten the beauty of all;
And only her soul has the magic to give it grace;
And only her hands have the cunning to put it in place.
Yes, the task that is given to each one, no other can do;
So the errand is waiting; it has waited through ages for you.

And now you appear; and the hushed ones are turning their
  gaze,
To see what you do with your chance in the chamber of days.

The technical help of my husband, Dr. Arthur Highman, in the preparation of the surveys and the statistical analyses of the responses, is gratefully acknowledged. I also wish to thank the many hundreds of individuals nationwide who were kind enough to participate in the surveys and interviews conducted. They freely unburdened themselves of both information and feelings, some of them buried and often intense. Also, the legal expertise of Louis and Bruce Highman in writing Chapter 12 has been most helpful.

Edith L. Highman

1

Introduction

Opportunities for career women have always been of special interest to me, for growing up in a male-dominated family I learned early that opportunities were not created equal for men and women. They still aren't.

I recently returned from a reunion of my high school class. The gathering reminded me of the many social changes that had taken place since the last time I had been a part of the group, almost half a century before. Those changes included a considerable one in the career status of women. It was a far different world for career women when I stepped before an audience in a Midwestern high school in June 1937 to deliver my commencement address about careers. The speech dealt with what was then a new trend in education, vocational guidance.

The high schools were beginning to initiate programs to offer students information about vocations and their requirements, to guide them in making successful and happy choices in selecting their careers.

The thought then was that we were living in an increasingly complex world, a world whose very complexity opened up an array of opportunities. To guide each student toward that work for which he or she was best fitted was to be one of the primary functions of the secondary school.

But in the 20,000 job classifications of the U.S. Census in that day, were the opportunities the same for women as for men?

Teaching, nursing, secretarial work were perceived to be the
desirable and available vocations for women, after high school,
and then only until marriage; after which, for the most part, a
woman's career was her home and her family. It was in World War
II that we saw the beginning of a radical change, when it became
necessary to recruit women for nontraditional occupations to fill
the ranks of workers needed in expanded factories, offices, and
government.

It seems to me that I have always been bucking what was con-
ventionally expected of me as a girl growing up in the twenties and
thirties. I grew up an only girl with four brothers. I must have been
seven years old when I informed my mother that I was probably
smarter than my brothers and I didn't see why I was the one who
had to help with the household chores just because I was the girl.
Of course it didn't do me much good. My mother was of the old
school, and quite horrified.

So at an early age I became very much aware of one form of
sex-related differentiation. It was not yet called male chauvinism. It
was simply the way things were.

Because I was very verbal and expressive as a child, I was given
the opportunity to take what were known as elocution lessons from
a Mrs. Harry Sherman who had been in Chautauqua, and was a
marvelous coach. Inspired by her, in the seventh grade I won first
place in the dramatic division of my school's declam contest. This
led to a further interest in interpretive reading, speech, and debate.
Going on into high school I had the opportunity of participating in
debate tournaments throughout the state of Iowa, and of winning a
few scholarships.

Following high school I spent a year at the State University in
anticipation of a traditional female vocation, teaching. But, un-
decided about teaching as a career, I completed a 9-month course in
a business school, and found myself in wartime Washington,
working in a stenographic pool in the Labor Department. This was
not where I wanted to stay—it was only a beginning and a challenge
to get ahead.

I managed to work myself out of the steno pool into a
secretarial position in the War Production Board. Then, because of
the shortage of male workers in wartime Washington, night classes

at the local university, and my ambitious nature, I maneuvered myself into a job as a correspondence clerk and then into a position as junior industrial analyst—without benefit of the usual requirement of a bachelor's degree, and despite the fact that I was female. In the office to which I was assigned as an analyst my two male colleagues were a graduate economist from a prominent southern university and an older businessman with considerable experience.

(What I experienced then is not uncommon today. Over half the organization women I surveyed started in clerical or secretarial work, and then went on to managerial and professional careers. A woman need not assume that as a clerk or secretary she can rise only to a higher-level clerkship or secretarial position. She can—with ambition, hard work, and further education and training—create a different and more challenging career.)

It was while working in the government bureaucracy that I first fully realized how strong were the feelings and biases of males about women in nonsecretarial positions. A man in the position of junior industrial analyst, considered to be a man's job, had female secretarial help to handle typing and clerical functions. But being the only woman working in a man's job, and a female with secretarial abilities, I was expected to do two jobs—the work of the analyst *plus* the typing and clerical functions. In other words, to make any progress I would do two jobs—the analytical and the secretarial. It was a man's world! (Even today, for a woman to be doing the equivalent of two jobs, "working twice as hard as a man," part of the price of upward progress, isn't unusual.)

The job of analyst involved the allocation of scarce materials to civilian industry in a wartime economy, following basic allocation priorities laid down by the War Production Board coordinating with the needs of the military services. Correspondence relating to such allocations would include the analyst's last name under "In reply refer to . . . " Telephone inquiries by those receiving the correspondence and allocations were referred to the responsible analyst. Always, for those cases referred to me, the voice at the end of the telephone assumed that he was to talk to Mr. . . . , and on hearing a feminine voice assumed I was the analyst's secretary, not the analyst.

Women have come a long way since World War II, in government and the professions and industry. There are now countless more opportunities. But what's behind an impressive facade of numbers of females now entering careers once denied them? What are the steps they must take to build their careers?

This book is about the role of sex-related perceptions, and other factors exclusive of ability and performance, in the taking of those steps. It relates specifically to women employed or hoping to be employed in large business organizations in management or in professional or in the better staff positions, and generally earning or aspiring to earn $25,000 to $100,000 and more annually (1982 dollars).

The book is based on information obtained from national surveys of random samples of organization women and men, principally executives and managers. This is supplemented by experience and observations over many years on how the people who run U.S. business and industry operate, and on what it takes for an individual to build a career in a large organization.

The men surveyed include corporate presidents, mostly vice presidents, other officers, some managers of operating and staff functions, and a few staff specialists and professionals (purchasing agent, analyst, etc.). The women include a considerable but lesser number of company officers; more managers (for the most part, in staff rather than in operating functions); and some specialists and professionals. Both women and men are employed principally in organizations which employ at least 1,000 people, and generally the largest corporations in the country. However, some women, and a very few men, are with smaller organizations.

Roughly 80 percent of the men are over forty years old, most of these over fifty. Just under half the women are over forty, and more of these in their forties than over fifty. The women generally earn over $25,000 annually, roughly half over $35,000. A majority of the women are married, 20 percent are single, 21 percent are separated or divorced, and 5 percent are widowed or are living with a man. Of the now-or-formerly married, one-third have children under eighteen and two-thirds do not.

Approximately 3,700 confidential questionnaires, covering an extensive list of items to be filled out and to be returned anonymously, unsigned, were mailed. Twenty-one percent of the women and eighteen percent of the men responded, generally filling out all questions, and with some exceptions generally without identification as to the respondent. By the cut-off date, 363 completed replies had been received from women and 306 from men. The returns have been tabulated, and the information received supplemented by in-depth personal interviews with the men who run their companies and the women who work with and for them.

Copies of the mail questionnaires used, and further details on the mailings and on those included in the survey, are to be found in the appendix (see page 150).

2

Factors in Building A Career—
Personal Qualities

Being a Hard Worker

A substantial proportion of the male executives surveyed in preparation for this book believe that most "organization" women in their firms, those earning $25,000 or more in 1982, work harder than do men in similar jobs and at similar responsibility levels. Only 2 percent of the men questioned believe most women work less hard than do their male counterparts. The great majority of women, as should be expected, concur in the view that the female works harder.

Interestingly, too, a considerable number of the male executives believe the women are more intelligent than the men in similar jobs; few believe them to be less intelligent. This is hardly surprising. The woman *does* mostly work harder than her male counterpart in the upper rungs of organizational society. She *has* to be a harder worker, and generally smarter than the man, to get to the same rung on the corporate ladder, and stay there, let alone progress. Because of discrimination against women it is the harder working and the more intelligent who are able to "make it" to the better-paying jobs—and then to a level of responsibility lower than that which the same hard work and intelligence would have brought them had they been men. One can't help thinking of the wonderful title of Derek A. Newton's book, *Think Like a Man, Act Like a Lady, Work Like a Dog.*

A San Francisco banker expounds on what it takes for a woman to get ahead in his bank: "A course in psychology, a course in patience, and she has to work harder than a man doing the same job." A Western newspaper editor, a woman, agrees that, "Before several promotions I had to work harder/longer and perform better than males in order to get the same degree of recognition." Yet also, in the words of a Chicago male executive, "Don't let trying too hard become evident to the point of showing tension—becoming shrill."

Women will work harder. It's the price of ambition, but the price can be exasperating. The managerial and professional woman resents it even while she does it. The chief financial officer of a Maine corporation vents her deeply felt resentment with the complaint of "having to put twice the effort into my job as a man and never getting any recognition . . . keeping my mouth shut and doing at least a 200 percent job effort in comparison to a man's 100 percent job effort." A California woman executive expresses this same feeling: "A woman has to work twice as hard as a man."

What can the aspiring career woman do about it? Nothing! Work harder and smarter! Don't let trying too hard become too evident, however. Don't forget that while working hard, being intelligent, and being productive helps in moving up the corporate hierarchy, particularly for a woman, there can be danger in being too obvious about it too. Out-working and out-shining others, too conspicuously making others look like slackers by comparison, can create enemies. Don't get too "shrill" too often about how hard you work.

Women are often perceived to be "shrill" or "abrasive" while men are merely "assertive." Quoting the president of a publishing firm, Carol Silberg, as reported in *U.S. News & World Report*[1]: "An aggressive quality in a woman is perceived as being bitchy—in a man, it's 'manly'."

Professional Attitude

The woman who wants to get ahead in a business firm has to start with a businesslike attitude. This means avoiding emotionalism, personalization of business decisions, undue sensitivity to criticism, pettiness, complaints, and gossip. It means conservative dress. It means not expecting special treatment because of being a woman; and avoiding undue emphasis on her sex, or playing sex games to gain favors, or as a substitute for ability and performance. It also means accepting the likelihood that in her organization there exists some degree of male chauvinism, discrimination, and unequal treatment, plus occasional sexual harassment; and learning to deal with their presence, up to a point—changing employers where the difficulties cannot be resolved.

She has to approach her job with an attitude of cooperation. "Fitting in" and getting along with her co-workers—bosses, peers, and subordinates—is vital. She has to recognize that she functions as a member of a "team" of co-workers. She does not work as a lone individual in the firm. She has to have a "company" attitude—a certain loyalty to the company and the company viewpoint.

Rosabeth M. Kanter[2] in describing the company she studied intensely, Industrial Supply Corporation (not its real name), refers to "fitting in" when she says of the corporation: "Emphasis was placed on getting along, 'keeping your nose clean,' and on having a smooth interpersonal style. Introspection was out. Intellectuals were suspect. Difficult or controversial subjects were avoided. . . . differences and anger were very difficult to express; instead, the atmosphere was expected to exemplify collaboration, agreement, and consensus. There were few, if any, rewards in fighting for something too hard or too openly [not universally true in organizations, however]. . . . team membership and getting along with peers [was important]. . . . 'Individual performers' were generally not promoted. . . . emotional expression . . . occurred through joking relationships. . . . having a good sense of humor also seemed to be a requisite for [upward] mobility."

To build a career a woman needs to project an image of objective unemotional professionalism on the job. This merits some emphasis. Fully 95 percent of the women responding to my surveys report to a man, only 5 percent to a woman. The male bosses they report to consider unemotional objectivity to be important. So do the women themselves. Fully half of all male executives queried in the national surveys conducted admit to perceiving the organization woman—the managerial and professional employee —as being more emotional than her male counterpart, and of the other half, it is inferred that a goodly portion join silently in the perception. This is the sex stereotype most widely held by male executives of the organization women who work for them.

The executive vice president of a Denver bank, alluding to problems faced in working with women, refers to "their emotional ups and downs;" and relevant to a woman's getting ahead, the importance of "presenting an unemotional objective image of technical and managerial competence."

A Boston executive concurs that "many career women can become emotional when involved in a difficult business situation." A Chicago official ascribes to some "a tendency to cry when angry or hurt." A Miami senior vice president believes that at least in part because they are emotional, organization women are "not willing to really follow through distasteful matters without help."

A Dallas human resources director points to "emotion interfering with making decisions." A Memphis executive expresses the opinion that "women are sometimes more given [than men] to letting emotion affect the job."

Career women themselves mention the excitability of the female. In the words of a female branch manager of a Minneapolis bank: "Women can be very emotional and also back-stabbing." The president of a Western firm, relative to problems she faces in working with women notes "their tendency to react emotionally to

business issues; their tendency to take business events personally."
A Los Angeles banker warns that a woman "must always be careful not to sound like an aggressive, emotional female. [It's frustrating] being compared to women who are emotional, irrational."

But a San Francisco industrial relations expert objects to "unconscious 'put-downs,' calling me emotional if angered; if men get angry—it's OK." A Cincinnati sales manager agrees: "Men don't view themselves as 'emotional,' yet label women as 'emotional' if they become the least excited. You constantly have to be on your guard." An engineering administrator similarly expresses her feeling that "it's a matter of interpreting the same behavior by men and women differently."

Women are considered to be too emotional to handle situations in business corporations, situations affecting dollars. They are not considered too emotional to be trusted with life and death situations in hospitals.

Whether women are really more emotional than men is less important than the perception that they are—by the male brass, and to a considerable degree by the women themselves.

How does a woman avoid being stereotyped as emotional? Regina Ryan and Janice LaRouche[3] suggest that she "cultivate a calm manner . . . [avoid] talk about your nerves, your anxiety, your depression, your moods. Talk is good therapy, but if you are seen as too emotional, you don't have that luxury at work . . . [avoid discussion of] psychosomatic ailments—ulcers, headaches, insomnia—and if you happen to be on any kind of medication, don't make it public. . . . Don't bring [associates] in on your personal problems. . . . "

Undue emotion interferes with the exercise of the objective rationality, decisions, and actions which promote the woman's career as well as the interests of her employer. The career woman "must always be careful not to sound like an aggressive emotional female." She must remember the importance of "presenting an unemotional objective image of technical and managerial competence." She must avoid emotion in a "difficult business situation." She should curb "a tendency to cry when angry or hurt." And whether she likes it or not, the successful career woman, like her male counterpart, must learn to "follow through distasteful matters without help." The woman who wants to get to the top cannot let emotion interfere with making decisions, or let personal dislikes of particular individuals interfere with working relationships which the job situation may demand. She's also going to have to avoid taking frustrating or unfair business events too personally.

On the last point, a conviction held almost as extensively as that on emotionalism, and by both men and women, is that the woman is more sensitive to criticism than the man. The belief is that women tend to view criticism very personally, not accepting it in a dispassionate objective way, or in a business context. Adverse criticism represents a personal put-down.

A Denver marketing executive sums it up with his opinion that "most women cannot take constructive criticism on a professional, nonemotional basis." Other male opinions include those of a Houston corporate officer who acquiesces in the belief that there is a "sensitivity to criticism;" and of a Pennsylvania vice president who claims a "tendency to 'personalize' decisions and conflicts." An Eastern company's general counsel agrees that women "personalize criticism," but also believes that to make matters worse they tend further to "automatically assume the critic is right [and that's sometimes not the case]."

Career women offer an additional slant. An Eastern public relations manager notes "the times when they (we) over-react and fail to be objective about a situation. I see the same reactions in minority males." A San Francisco executive on problems she encounters in working with women alludes to their "being over-sensitive to any comment or action by men that can be construed as discriminatory."

What all this amounts to is that a woman on the way up has simply got to develop a thick skin, even thicker than an upwardly mobile man's. She is going to face more criticism than will a man, if she's able enough and aggressive enough to push herself ahead. She is going to meet discrimination, condescension, comments, and gibes that really *are* personal, because she's a woman. Too, she will be resented by other women, jealous of her success.

A thick skin is also a prerequisite, along with interpersonal sensitivity, in the distasteful side of an organization woman's duties, that comes with line management particularly, less so with staff work—the reprimand, discipline, and when necessary the lay-off of subordinates.

Firing can be particularly hard when it has to be done to competent people whom the woman manager has worked with for a long time and whom she personally likes. Lay-offs may be required to meet a budget when business is slow; or even when business is good, to show how good a manager she is by improving efficiency—cutting costs, i.e., cutting out people—or to follow direct orders from her boss. There is no getting around such facts of business life, and she has to nerve herself to live with them.

A career woman will need to be able to cope with the crises that arise from time to time in her role as a manager or professional. Over one-third of the male executives surveyed voice the belief that a woman is less able than a man to cope with a crisis. This belief is consistent with views on the emotionalism of women. Cool objectivity, of course, is likely to be more useful than emotion in the stress of a crisis.

As for stress, fully 20 percent of the organization women surveyed answered "yes" to the question: "Is increase in job stress with career advancement likely to deter me in the future from seeking additional promotions?" Of course some male managers too would answer "yes," but probably not 20 percent would *admit* to such a fear.

Some quotes by the men surveyed on the career woman's ability to cope with crises and stress are provocative. A young Dallas financial officer believes without question that career women "are generally too emotional and unlikely to be able to cope well with high stress situations." An older Indiana director of industrial and employee relations insists similarly that women "react poorly when under stress." A Texas director of management development refers to career women's "inability to take high job pressure." Finally, another executive (obviously a male chauvinist) expounds: "Anyone can steer a ship in calm waters, but can women do it in troubled waters?"

What should a woman do in a crisis? Keep cool. That's a trait which simply has to be learned. Handling a crisis is in large part a matter of emotion control.

The organization woman needs to be self-confident. She also needs to be decisive. This does not mean self-confidence to the point of arrogance; or decisiveness to the point of either acting without aforethought, or in the face of changing circumstance, refusing to change a decision once made.

Many women lack the self-confidence they need. They do not completely trust their own abilities and tend to be intimidated by the male. There is at times an acceptance of inferior status and that the female cannot compete effectively with the male because she is "only a woman." The "clerk" mentality, so often engendered by a woman's entry job in the business world, needs to be opened up if one is to build a career as a manager or a professional.

Korn/Ferry International, an executive search firm, jointly with the University of California at Los Angeles (UCLA) graduate school of management, conducted a survey of 300 women at the level of vice president and above in a sampling of the largest corporations in the U.S. The foremost career obstacle cited was that of "being a woman." (See the discussion of male chauvinism in Chapter 4.) The second most frequently mentioned obstacle was *"lack of confidence."*[4]

Self-confidence is important. The president and owner of a privately held moderately large candy manufacturing company died a few years ago. The widow, uninterested herself in taking over the presidency, was faced with a choice between two vice presidents, Susan Childs and Dorothy Field. On being interviewed Susan *knew* she could handle the job and said so. Dorothy *thought* she could, but wanted a few days to think about it. Neither was really ready for the top spot, but Susan apparently had more confidence in herself and her ability to learn quickly on the job. Susan was picked, and while she had a few scary moments in her first months as president, she did learn, and succeed. Self-confidence paid off.

Decisiveness

What about being decisive? Under pressure of time and circumstance decisions frequently have to be made without all of the facts being known. The known must be supplemented with general experience, guesswork and even "intuition" (sometimes another word for experience). The woman manager often does not have the luxury of waiting for all the facts bearing on a situation before she must make a decision. Some of the facts cannot be known beforehand in any case.

This brings to mind the considerable difference in the decision-making process between the "researcher" (or somewhat akin, the professional, or the *staff* manager) and the *line* manager. The "research" mind is trained to think in terms of assembling and analyzing all the available objective facts of a situation, and then recommending a decision to someone else who carries the actual responsibility for it. The *line* manager knows a decision must be reached, with a time limit, often without all the facts. Further, the line manager must give due weight to the intangible *"people"* relationships so often involved in a decision, as well as the *objective* facts. And she carries the personal responsibility for what happens as a result of her decision.

That is why the "research" trained individual—or the professional or the individual with staff rather than line management experience—when promoted to a line manager's job often turns out to be inadequate for that job. Similarly, a good line manager may produce poor results when moved to staff duties. Some individuals can be very good at both line and staff work, but most are unlikely to be exceptionally good at both.

A further note on decision making. It's well to remember that either delaying a decision or making no decision at all is itself a decision. If one hesitates and delays investing in stocks, that's a decision in itself, just as much as is a decision to invest now. If one is indecisive about the unpleasant managerial chore of firing someone, then that's actually a decision to retain that worker, at least until one decides otherwise. If one can't decide whether to change the price of a product she's selling, or whether to buy a computer, or to switch to a new supplier for a raw material, she's actually made decisions to delay action until such time as she decides otherwise. *No decision* is always itself a *decision.*

Male executives tend to believe that women are less decisive than men. This view is shared by at least some of the women surveyed. If women are indeed less decisive than their male counterparts, that would be consistent with the old adage about women finding it hard to make up their minds, or the right of a woman to change her mind.

Cultural factors may play a role in indecisiveness. In their upbringing women presumably still are widely taught by society, and industry, that men and not women make the important decisions in the work place. Male stereotyping of female decision making is consistent with conventional belief that a woman feels more intensely than a man the need for security. The woman therefore tends to avoid the risks inherent in making decisions which could turn out to be wrong. "I'd better not stick my neck out!" "Which way do I decide, to minimize my risk? Never mind also the question of which way is best for the firm; minimizing risk is best for *me.*" "Maybe I can stall a little longer on a decision, or get it taken out of my hands." But then one has to consider, too—if a man makes a wrong decision he can be forgiven; a woman is less likely to be.

Male views on women's decisiveness are illustrated by the statement of a senior vice president of one of our very largest U.S. corporations. He refers to women's "unwillingness to take a firm position on difficult issues." The male marketing director of a New Jersey firm likewise explains that "some women have a fear of making decisions without confirmation."

A similar perspective on women's decisiveness is held by many of the organization women themselves. A Southern California financial controller expresses a belief that "most women have difficulty confronting face to face on a problem and resolving it. They prefer going to a male counterpart who only pacifies them." An engineering executive alleges that in her experience women "can't make decisions, need too many details." A product marketing manager comments on a common problem her sex has, "overanalyzing one's own decisions."

But, interestingly, a female department head in the garment industry claims " 'typical female' behavior (mind-changing) is *helpful*—in this industry. Perhaps it is more accepted because industry is female-oriented.''

Decisiveness and the appearance of decisiveness are very important. At the same time the managerial and professional female must be aware of the need to be flexible, and of the need to compromise at times. She may have to fight for her ideas more than would a man. She may feel it necessary sometimes to be assertive to the point of appearing to be obstinate, just to show that she is an equal with her male peers. Yet an able manager or professional *will* change course if conditions change, or if additional facts bearing on a course of action come to light. The female must remember that there is need in an enterprise for compromise, even at times for compromise with mediocrity, discouraging as this may be to innovation and creativity. And the greater the size of the enterprise, the greater is the need for compromise.

It's also appropriate to point out that what constitutes inflexibility to one person may well be decisiveness (or firmness and strength, self-confidence, determination, perseverance) to another.

On the whole, male executives consider women to be neither more nor less inflexible than men. A few, however, do rate women as the more obstinate. A New York vice president observes: ''As the facts for a particular problem change women seem to be less flexible in altering their views.'' A second male, from Northern California, believes women show a ''lack of flexibility as they grow older.'' [Unlike men?] A third male executive notes a ''tendency of women to express insecurity through aggressiveness and domineering style, inflexibility and less willingness [than men] to compromise.'' A Miami female vice president similarly complains of women's ''*inflexibility* and unwillingness to adapt to changes.''

Being Organized

A good manager or professional ought to be reasonably well organized in her work. Noting this, one should also note that women generally are better organized than their male colleagues.

At least that's what a major portion of male executives, the bosses, think.

This is not surprising. Men are more accustomed to shunting off the organization of details to assistants and secretaries than are women. Indeed, many career women worked their way up the ranks by doing the "grunt" work thus shunted off, and organizing it for the men.

There is some evidence also that men feel more confident than do women about "winging it," the impromptu approach, in discussing a situation in a meeting with associates, in explaining a proposal to the boss, or in making a presentation to a client. Women are inclined to feel less confident of the extemporaneous way. They are therefore more needful of and more practiced in organized preparation. Perhaps that simply is a facet of a greater need for security assurance and a lesser propensity for risk-taking.

The female president of a California company commenting on men states: "They seem less well organized . . . compared with women." The woman marketing manager of a Boston firm says of men: "They are far less organized, lose papers, forget things, work sloppy." A New York director of marketing services, referring to her problems in working with men, criticizes "their lack of organizational skills" and lack of "attention to detail."

Quality-mindedness in work/product output is another desirable characteristic of good managers and professionals. On this score too the male executive perceives women to rank better than their male counterparts. This may be related to being better organized, and to paying more attention to detail. Good quality also may be related to a fear that poor quality hurts the job security to which women appear more sensitive than men. Too, quality sometimes is a matter of patience, and perhaps women through necessity have had more practice than men in being patient.

Practicality

A practical outlook plus knowledge and skill at the job are essential in building a career. Here, women are at some disadvantage. Many male bosses view women as less practical than men.

This is an image perhaps created in part because women have been less exposed to things mechanical than have men in their up-bringing. It also is undoubtedly tied in with beliefs in the greater emotionalism of women.

In reality, women may be the more practical of the sexes in their outlook on matters that directly affect them. In love and in choosing a marriage partner it is often thought to be the woman who tends to be practical, the man the romantic. And on a different level, in the everyday business of shopping for groceries it is apt to be the woman who tends to be more value-conscious than the man.

The male executive may have some basis, however, for reservations about women's practicality on the basis of degree of exposure and experience. Women have not yet had as extensive exposure as men to technical/business education nor to managerial and professional experience. When—albeit infrequently—a woman with really inadequate preparation and experience is placed in a position beyond her capacity because of a need to show adherence to an affirmative action program, the adverse results color the male's impressions of managerial and professional women.

Women's representation in technical fields and in the business schools of our universities is growing, but is still that of a minority. (According to *Statistical Abstracts of the United States, 1984*[5] women accounted for roughly 10 percent of all engineering degrees and for 25 percent of all MBA degrees granted in 1981.) Women's experience too has been limited generally to lower level supervision or management, and to *staff* positions (specialists, aides, "assistants to"), rather than in *line* (command) positions. In confirmation, three-fourths of the male executives surveyed claimed that the better-paid women hold mainly staff, not line positions in their companies, and review of the jobs held by the women surveyed reinforces the claim.

It is only recently that women have penetrated, to a limited degree, middle and upper middle management levels (mostly staff), and to a *very* limited degree, higher management levels (either line or staff).

The limitations of female experience are specifically referred to in the commentary of a number of male executives. The corporate controller of a large San Francisco-based organization explains that women "lack experience due to the relatively short time during which women have been offered managerial positions in nontraditional fields." The senior vice president of a major savings and loan company claims career women suffer a "lack of experience that leads to top jobs, ([because] women haven't worked in some businesses long enough)."

A Grand Rapids, Michigan executive points out that women have a "lack of [line] management or supervisory experience since most enter through staff positions." A Californian refers to this absence of line experience in his company: "The tradition [holds] that certain positions are male positions—generally line operations."

Similarly, the vice president of a manufacturing firm speaks of women's "lack of experience in certain business activities such as manufacturing [line]." A Dayton, Ohio vice president also refers to "male tradition—we have a few women in management in junior supervisory positions—none in major line positions."

A couple of female comments too are in order. A woman executive in public relations complains that "men in positions of power in my company still don't consider women for promotions to officer level. [In my company] there are only five out of 150 middle management people who are women in my [middle management] status." A marketing manager for a paper products company claims that in her firm "most of the really significant operational jobs women are not as yet considered for."

The female vice president of a Chicago bank points to a sticky problem regarding top jobs, the "lack of women in higher management levels to 'prove' that women can do the job. Women have been very successful at lower management levels and [therefore many other] women were [consequently] promoted into those [lower] positions [because of the success of the first ones]."

Being "practical" is commonly the result of experience. The lack of relevant practical experience in line management, and in the upper levels of management, really *can* lead to impracticality. In a sense this is a Catch-22 situation for the woman.

The perception of the male boss (and most bosses are male), as to women's practical sense is a handicap that can be overcome. It's by no means a universal perception by the male, but a woman should be aware of it. Be extra careful not to be too impulsive about trying out a new idea. Check it out first for its practicality by thinking it through in all its aspects yourself. Discuss it with others informally. Test it out on a small scale if this can be done. *Then* try it out on the boss. But being "extra careful" unfortunately can be dangerous too if it stifles innovative thinking. Catch-22 again!

Other Assets

How does one gain knowledge and skill at the job, beyond what comes with tenure (time spent) in the job? The ambitious woman will take courses, attend seminars, attend trade and professional meetings, "read up," and cultivate those who can be helpful with information and advice on matters bearing on her current job. The same is equally important in respect to her hoped-for future jobs. Nor should the woman be stinting of personal time in doing these things. If her career is *really* her prime priority, she won't.

In respect to a number of desirable characteristics not yet mentioned women tend to get higher marks than do men, judging from the responses of male corporate executives. Thus women are considered to be more considerate and diplomatic (but less devious) than men. They are also held to be more honest, less likely from the viewpoint of the boss to "shade," cover up, or distort the facts of a situation in reporting to the boss. And they are held to be less ruthless than men. In most cases ruthlessness is not in the long run the most productive way of managing people.

3

Managerial Traits

Aggressiveness

For the woman who would rise in an organizational hierarchy that is largely male a certain amount of aggressiveness is essential. *Ability* to rise is not enough. There must be the *will* to rise, or the will must be developed. And for the woman who wants to get ahead as a line manager (command) in her organization, rather than as a specialist or "assistant to" (staff, e.g., advisory) there must be a will to boss.

Just how aggressive is the career woman? The top executives of our largest U.S. business enterprises believe organization women and men are generally about equally aggressive. An undertone, however, in the replies received from male executives indicates that top management is a bit more sensitive to female than to male over-aggressiveness. In the words of career consultant Lawrence D. Schwimmer[6] this may at least in part be due to "a mind-set on the part of many men who aren't used to women being vocal and communicating honestly and directly [in office communication]. Many men will view that kind of assertive behavior as aggressive. So women must know the fine line between being pushy and a pushover to be effective in getting things done and getting cooperation from others."

The male director of government affairs for a San Francisco company points out that in response to discrimination and "prejudice, some women (a few) have developed abrasive personalities." (In males it might be called "assertive?") Another male, a Detroit vice president, is irritated by women "when they attempt to emulate the actions of and mannerisms of their male counterparts, i.e., rough language, etc., and in addition over-aggressiveness in the job function." The women surveyed, as opposed to men, more often seem to be concerned that the female be more aggressive in "standing up for herself;" and to be less accepting of "pats on the head."

A San Francisco woman complains of "women's lack of assertiveness and acceptance of inferior status." Another organization woman likewise observes that women are not willing to stand up for themselves.

A good many organization women feel that not only women in general, but more specifically they themselves are lacking in adequate assertiveness. Yet occasionally one finds a woman like a Montgomery, Alabama vice president who is irritated by other females who feel that "they must constantly assert themselves—take everything as a 'put-down' on women—always on the defensive."

Some degree of assertiveness is necessary for the woman who wants to get ahead, even if it be what one male executive calls "controlled" assertiveness. He defines this as "striking a balance in the relationship between deference and overcompensating aggressiveness."

What are some guidelines for "controlled" assertiveness? To start with, the organization woman should make sure her mentor(s) (see Chapter 6) and others in influential positions somehow learn of what she's done, when it's something important, and has been done well. She should not brag about her accomplishments continually, nor belittle them either. She should apologize, if need be, for something done less well; but not repetitively. She should speak up at meetings when the opportunity presents itself, particularly at staff and other meetings which include her boss, but not to excess. The organization woman should back up her superior where appropriate. She may oppose his ideas but tactfully and usually privately being wary of criticizing his ideas publicly. The following illustrates the point.

The senior vice president of a large consumer products firm at times conducted "skip-level" meetings. When he had to reach an important decision involving expenditure in the field, and wasn't sure that he had gotten *all* the facts from immediate subordinates, he would call a meeting of field personnel. These were the subordinates of the headquarters managers who reported directly to him. The executive believed that talking with them confidentially, in the absence of their bosses, would provide more completely and more accurately the "unfiltered" information he wanted. He therefore would "skip" one level of management (the headquarters group) and review a particular situation directly with the submanagers in the field.

At one such meeting Mary Russell spoke up, strongly expressing views that were in opposition to those of her boss at headquarters. Anything discussed in the meeting and the views expressed were supposed to be confidential. Unfortunately, whenever such a meeting involves a number of people, "confidential" does not necessarily remain so. Mary's boss heard about her expressed views. Thereafter, the good relations Mary had had with him deteriorated rapidly. Assertively speaking in opposition to her superior's views to his boss, in the presence of others in a multi-person meeting, was misplaced assertiveness which courted risk, and was an error. Mary could have been properly assertive and differed with her boss, tactfully to his face, but not to others, and particularly not to her boss's boss and in the presence of others.

The organization woman should keep the boss informed of what she is doing on the job. Where appropriate, she may seek to consult with him for advice on assignments from time to time. It flatters him. But she should not overdo it.

She needs to control her temper. It may be vented occasionally, but only deliberately, when it serves a purpose. One example: with a subordinate when the subordinate has done work for a higher-echelon executive or for one of her peers without first clearing with her. To protect her sphere of authority, she may also have to remonstrate, either tactfully or forcefully, as called for, with the higher executive or her peer for not going through authority channels—herself. However, judgment is needed as to where and when bypassing authority is customary in the organization.

The managerial and professional may complain to her boss when necessary, but not continually. She needs to be careful about voicing complaints to her boss' peers or to the boss' boss.

The organization woman should be sure her boss is aware that she expects to build a career in the company, and to progress upward with time. She should keep her eyes and ears open for promotion opportunities. When one occurs, her boss ought to be informed she wants it. If successful in getting the promotion, she should speak up if the salary increase is not appropriate to the position. If unsuccessful, she ought to try for an understanding that she'll get the next promotion available. (This assumes she's better qualified than competitors). If one doesn't get a promotion or a salary increase, threatening to quit is unwise unless one is prepared to do so. Negotiation is a better course.

Sarah Lewis was one of seven professionals assigned to a new unit in a financial institution. All had similar positions and were at the same professional level. All used the same typing pool to get out correspondence and reports. Sarah was the only woman in the group of seven, and her work was always the last to get typed. (Women, typists among them, often resent other women, especially those in positions higher than their own). It was not until Sarah finally spoke to her boss about it—asserted herself—that the situation was rectified—3 months later.

Some women have gone up the corporate ladder without ever having to ask for a promotion; or so they claim. For most, however, experience indicates that promotions have to be asked for. Asking can at least expedite advancement.

The divisional merchandising manager of a retail organization, John Mason, was promoted to the job of general merchandising manager. He selected his successor from among his three assistant divisional merchandise managers, Sue, Bill, and Harold. Sue was recognized as the most capable of the three. Bill was capable, but less so. Harold was the youngest and still limited in experience. Bill was the one picked. Sue had hoped for the job, and had she asked for it she would not have been refused. But she was deferential, and the man who got it was aggressive. He asked for the job; she did not. John Mason had simply assumed that he was to pick a man for what had hitherto in that organization been a man's job. He really hadn't realized Sue wanted it. She had never discussed her ambitions with him. More assertiveness on Sue's part would have helped.

A young woman engineer working as a draftsman for a large industrial construction company noted after 2 years that one male colleague after another in her group, hired right after graduation as she was, had been promoted to more advanced design work. She had not. She had never really let her boss know that she harbored ambitions that went beyond drafting alone. She finally did speak to her boss about it. Three months later when the opportunity presented itself she got her promotion. It could have come earlier had she spoken up sooner.

Promotions commonly, though not always, have to be requested. Merit increases in salary in the same job, not a promotion, in large organizations with codified salary schedules, mostly don't have to be requested. They're automatic, though even so, bargaining for a specific level of classification within a position, and thus the amount of an increase, sometimes is helpful. With smaller firms it may be necessary to ask for even merit raises.

When the timing is right, as when a woman has done something especially well that contributes to or protects a department's or division's performance, her boss' reputation with his boss, and/or the company profits, she should ask for a promotion or a raise. A check on what males at her level of responsibility in the organization are getting, if it can be made, and on what size of raises are being given, is useful. She should consider what her contributions to the department or division and the company have been, and also the sales and profit picture for her group and the company. Asking for too little is a mistake. So is asking for something excessive. However, asking for more than she expects to get may be advisable. But in asking, picking an opportune moment is important.

A food manufacturer had a problem. A batch of product which had been contaminated was inadvertently shipped out to its supermarket customers. The spoiled product did not make people sick, but its taste was awful. The amount of product affected was substantial, and the complaints would certainly hurt the company with both the supermarkets and consumers. A meeting was held of the top corporate executives plus the manufacturing and marketing personnel most directly involved. The product needed to be recalled, but publicizing the real reason—contamination and taste—was not going to be helpful. A number of alternative suggestions were discussed, none of them satisfactory. Finally Sylvia, an assistant product sales manager, suggested the shipments could be recalled on the basis that the transparent plastic packaging material, for the particular product batch involved, was likely to develop an unattractive yellowish tone on the grocery shelves within a short time. On that basis the spoiled product was immediately recalled, largely even before it went from supermarket warehouses (to where it had been shipped) to the grocery shelves. The damage to the food manufacturer was minimized. It could have been very costly.

Sylvia was an instant heroine. She was also underpaid. She was also not assertive. This was the opportune moment for her to ask for a promise of a promotion to a job as product manager as soon as one became available. (She knew one of the managers was leaving for another job soon). It was also the moment to ask for an immediate raise in the meantime in her present job. She would have received both. She asked for neither, and 3 months later, when the emergency that made her a heroine had largely been forgotten, she did not get the product manager's job that opened up. Nor did she, 6 months later, get more than half the raise she could have gotten earlier, immediately, even without a promotion.

Helen Field was a legal assistant in a law firm. During the course of her work on a case involving an important client, a transportation company, she learned a great deal about that client. She also met the head of the client company when bringing over some documents to be signed. Later it occurred to her that there were some problems with the public and with customers which the company was not meeting as well as it should. She thought she knew what ought to be done about those problems. Being assertive and willing to risk her employer's displeasure she contacted the man she had met, the president of the transportation company, and discussed her ideas. The upshot of her aggressiveness? Helen is now vice president of public relations for the transportation company. She started with one person in a department consisting solely of herself, and built rapidly from there. At the law firm she would have remained a legal assistant.

One often has more leverage in asking for authority, salary, and title when first asked to join an organization than later. Then is the time to be assertive, though nicely, in requesting what one considers are reasonable demands. If one can't get them then, or a reasonable facsimile, maybe one doesn't want what's being offered.

Some authorities believe a secretary's job is a dead-end job, permanently consigning a woman to a minor subservient function in an organization. This need not be true if she is assertive enough to make it clear to her boss that she does not expect to remain a secretary. If she undertakes to prepare herself for advancement through courses at the local university or otherwise, she should publicize that too. If she has good rapport with the man or woman she works for she can learn a great deal about the company by observing and asking intelligent questions. If the one she's working for is at a fairly high level in the organization, she is in a position to know more about its workings than do the managers who report to her boss. She is likely to be more aware than others of company goals, directions, and politics.

With tact, she can offer suggestions about situations referred to in company reports, memos, and correspondence that flow through her hands. She can learn about and get acquainted with the people who come to see her boss, or with whom she makes appointments for her boss.

A secretary can learn before others do of opportunities which may arise that she could fill. If her boss considers her to be intelligent and knows she is ambitious and is doing something to prepare herself for promotion, she's got a good chance to move into an advantageous spot when it opens up. She can go up from there. It is interesting to note that fully 18 percent of the managerial and professional women surveyed started with their present employer as a secretary.

The degree of assertiveness appropriate for a woman depends on the job, the boss, the situation, and the company. As an example, one insurance company encourages assertiveness to the point of freely going over the head of the boss; and speaking up with one's own ideas in meetings in opposition to the opinions of the boss, even with the boss' peers and superiors present. In most other companies in the same and other industries that would be misplaced assertiveness which would be sure to get one fired, promptly.

Assertiveness is encouraged by confidence in the ability to transfer to another boss in the organization, if need be; or to get another job with a new employer which is at least as good as the present one. To provide such confidence, mentors and networking, discussed in Chapter 6, are helpful. To some degree, assertiveness also correlates with the amount of financial and psychological support and encouragement a woman can expect from her personal savings account and her spouse.

Linked with assertiveness is a willingness to take on responsibility. The male executives surveyed feel that women managers are willing to take on new responsibilities more readily than do men. This is a plus for the ambitious woman—so long as it doesn't merely mean the boss thinks a woman can more easily be pressured into taking on new job burdens without added personnel to carry them out. Male managers may be more insistent that with new responsibility should come a bigger budget.

The willingness to take on new responsibilities, or to seek them out, is reflected in the fact that fully 15 percent of the organization women surveyed claim to have created their current jobs.

A willingness to take on new responsibilities implies a willingness to take on a new job when a company decision or promotion requires it. A new job often means a move to a new location. Especially for the woman who is married this could mean some difficulties. Considerations of personal versus company priorities are reviewed in Chapter 11.

Somewhat related to assertiveness or aggressiveness is arrogance. Just a touch of this exists among some women, not many, who have been promoted to the better jobs. A Youngstown marketing vice president expresses his belief that women "tend to be impressed with a little responsibility which creates an impression of arrogance." A Boston manager says that "promotions sometimes go to their heads . . . feeling that as a promoted woman she does not still have to be considerate" [express proper deference to the male?]. An Illinois executive gives his opinion: "Some become overbearing upon their successful advancement."

Male comments on arrogance may to a degree really reflect the irritation of male chauvinists at the progress women have made. But, there could be a bit of fire where there's smoke. Quoting one woman manager, the "female managerial bitch, [just as the male martinet] is not an unknown." The upwardly mobile woman ought to try to avoid giving the impression of arrogance, even while trying to maintain self-assertion.

I am reminded of the woman engineer working in a defense industry where personnel are shifted from time to time to different projects as old contracts expire or new ones are received. Each project has its own project manager. With shifts from one project to another the people one works with change, as does the boss. The young engineer remarked in an interview: "One never goes out of the way to antagonize someone, because one never knows whom she will be working with, or for, or when." Arrogance is one way of antagonizing others.

The newly appointed head of a company's accounting department was a young woman who had come up fast in the organization since she was hired on graduation from a prestigious university business school. Just a touch of arrogance had come with her MBA degree. A rapid series of promotions was fostered by the company's need to conform with affirmative action quotas. The young MBA chose to believe the advancement merely confirmed her exceptional ability. With the new promotion as head of the accounting department her touch of arrogance really blossomed. The contrast in style with the former manager who had retired was sharp, and the subordinates were keenly aware of it.

The department was a closely knit group who had worked well together for a number of years. Under the former manager, when occasion required it, individuals had voluntarily worked overtime to keep current and get work out on time without being specifically required to do so. Under the new manager this changed. The 5:00 p.m. quitting time now was strictly adhered to by everyone, at all times, except as the new manager specifically demanded overtime. However, the new manager wasn't always voluntarily informed by her subordinates sufficiently ahead of time about when overtime was needed. Passive resistance slows things down too. Report deadlines began to be missed. The error rate went up. Several people quit. And finally a new manager was brought in to head the department.

Caroline and Stella were peers in a food manufacturing concern. Caroline was assistant marketing manager for Group A products. Stella held the same position for Group B products. They were friendly. Then Caroline was promoted to the position of marketing manager for her group. It represented a considerable step up in salary as well as position. Stella remained an assistant marketing manager. The promotion went to Caroline's head, and the friendship with Stella cooled. Stella felt snubbed and resented it. Somewhat later a reorganization occurred. Group B's marketing manager was fired, Groups A and B were consolidated, and Stella, who had been assistant manager for B, became head of marketing for the combined group. Caroline now reported to Stella—and shortly thereafter left the company. Arrogance *can* backfire.

Articulating

The ability to articulate and communicate is important to upward movement in the corporate world. This is stressed by both male and female executives and managers. On this score women are believed to do better than their male counterparts by a goodly portion of the men surveyed. This opinion is consistent with widely held views that girls are brought up to be more language-oriented, "talky-talky," than are boys. The importance of the characteristic is especially emphasized by the numbers of women who insist that to get ahead in their firms "the ability to communicate well—speaking and writing" is essential.

Males feel the same way. A corporate personnel director notes the importance to a woman of "the ability to communicate in groups as well as with peers." Other comments by male executives point out the importance of an "ability to communicate with people at all levels;" and "communicating results of job performance" (i.e., don't be bashful—let the boss know, in an unobnoxious way of course, how good you are).

An ability to articulate and communicate is basic to the ability to persuade and to sell. This applies to the selling of a company's products and services but also to selling one's ideas, programs and reports, or oneself—to superiors, peers, and subordinates, to customers, and to prospective employers, or to others within and outside one's organization. Both the ability to speak well to one person or to many, and the ability to write well are important.

Motivating

One of the most important characteristics an ambitious woman must possess is the ability to motivate the people who report to her. This is discussed at length in Chapter 5 on dealing with subordinates.

Risk-taking

Part of a manager's job is a willingness to take actions which involve risk. The "calculated" risk may be in terms of whether a new computer setup requiring a large capital investment will really do the job it's supposed to do. The risk may lie in whether money invested in an unusual advertising campaign or in new types of promotion effort will pay off in actual sales results. A manager in approving the manufacture of a new product is gambling on its acceptance in the marketplace. And a bank officer in approving a loan which is highly profitable to her bank also runs the risk of a considerable loss to the bank if the loan recipient's business plans go awry. Risks are to both the employer and the manager's career.

Over one-third of the male bosses to whom women managers report perceive the woman to be less willing to take a calculated risk than is her male counterpart. Only 4 percent believe her to be more willing than the man to take such risks. This perception is a handicap to the progress of women in management, insofar as there are times when risks *must* be taken. This is particularly true in line management. (It is line which makes decisions, staff which advises. Most women managers are staff. As such, they have relatively limited need for, and therefore limited experience, in the taking of calculated risks for the employer).

Many of the managerial and professional women who have been queried agree that women are more risk-averse than are their male counterparts. It is likely that as women gain more experience in the corporate hierarchy they will be fully as willing to take calculated risks as are men. Overcoming a fear of taking risks is to some degree a matter of self-confidence. This in turn comes with experience. A willingness to take risks is also increased, as is assertiveness, by one's perception of the likelihood of being able to get a good job elsewhere if need be, by money in the bank, and by the financial and psychological support of a spouse.

The calculated risk is taken with greater confidence if a woman has evaluated the pros and cons of a risky course of action, and the likely size of the risk versus the likely size of the benefits. Discussion of the factors involved with her boss, mentors, network contacts, and others in whom she has confidence can help. (The very fact that she has talked it over with her boss minimizes the personal risk if an action she has proposed turns out badly). The more facts about a situation which she has, the less the risk of a wrong judgment or action. If you can test an idea or action on a small scale first you minimize risk.

Where a risk is involved as to performance when investing in a relatively new type of office equipment, information can be sought on the experience others have had with the same equipment. The experience of others can likewise be sought to minimize the risk of other losses, such as on bank loans or trade credit extended to a specific customer.

A calculated risk sometimes takes the form of a decision by a manager to go ahead with an innovation or an investment for which she should, but deliberately has not, first gotten approval from her superiors. For a discussion and an example see Chapter 8 on understanding the boss.

In some situations a manager who takes no risks takes the greatest risk of all, for then obsolete equipment, new forms of competition, and deteriorating sales and profits may assure failure and the severance of employment.

Delegating

A manager must delegate to her subordinates the work to be done. She cannot do it all herself, nor is it her business to attempt to do so. Here again, as with the calculated risk, some male executives (25 percent) perceive a woman to be less willing to delegate than a man.

That some male executives believe the man more easily delegates is understandable, if one assumes a woman is less willing than a man to take risks. There are risks involved in delegating to a subordinate. To a manager the subordinate is "obviously" less competent than herself (most superiors feel superior). The manager's future promotability or even her job may be at risk if a subordinate less competent than herself turns out poor work where quality is important. If the work is *very* important a strong desire for security may lead to special reluctance to risk the future on the output of a subordinate whose competence she doesn't completely trust. Also tied in may be the thought: "Why do too good a job training a subordinate in all of the details of my job through full delegation of the work to be done, if that subordinate then can some day replace me?"

Of course, there are risks in *not* adequately delegating—not getting the work out; getting oneself so loaded with work that quality suffers; inadequate time to think, plan, and supervise; inadequate time to prepare for one's hoped-for next promotion; and no time for "political" defense or offense in aiming for promotion. And one of the best ways for a woman to keep from getting promoted is *not* to have someone trained to replace her in her present job. See Chapter 5 for a more detailed discussion of delegation.

Politics

Aside from being *qualified* for promotion, *political savvy* is important to progress in the management hierarchy. This is especially true in large organizations. "Understanding how an organization works and building a solid relationship with those in decision-making positions" is the way one career woman expresses it. "Making correct political assessments" is the phrase used by another. Other remarks by executive women summarize the political requirements in the following words: "Understanding corporate politics and corporate long-range goals;" "playing politics and coming out on the winning side;" "becoming politically attuned to 'good old boy' network—learning to work within it;" "working for the 'right' people;" "knowing the right people and socializing with upper management males;" "the ability to successfully stroke some powerful people—with larger than normal egos;" and "making sure good job performance is noted through contacts with executives in important positions."

One must be careful, of course, to avoid antagonizing one's immediate boss, or others, by making political ploys too obviously or too often. For example, a male executive emphasizes that a woman must avoid being characterized as "tending to 'discuss' problems innocently with superiors above her direct supervisor."

Organizational politics are important, and like it or not, the woman who wants to get ahead in her organization should be aware of political considerations if she's going to climb the corporate ladder. The following may be helpful.

1. Determine what your goals are.

2. Be mindful of image, or of how people perceive you. When first starting on a job, if you can arrange it so, being introduced to your peers and subordinates by the boss himself is better than being introduced by somebody from the personnel office, or by an unpopular peer, or by your chief's subordinate. Getting started in a company at a high level and at a high salary is better than starting at a low level or salary. This is why one may prefer to turn down a low salary in one company, hoping that with additional time and effort she may secure a higher starting salary elsewhere. Getting

started in the sales department in a company where all top jobs are filled by people who have come up through sales is better, where you have a choice, as on completing a management training program, than starting in accounting if very few top jobs are filled from people in accounting. This assumes you like both sales and accounting.

3. Consider what's important in getting ahead in the organization. If publishing is more important than teaching and working with students in getting promoted on a college campus, concentrate on publishing. If duck hunting as a hobby is an essential to upward progress in a company headed by a duck-hunting fanatic who's likely to remain head for many years, then if you plan to stay and progress in that company you had better become a duck hunter. Otherwise change your plans and get a job elsewhere.

4. Develop a support system for yourself, starting with the boss. Develop one or preferably more mentors. It happens that most often within a company the boss is the one or principal mentor. If circumstances permit, supplement the boss with other influentials in and out of the company. Build a network of useful contacts. Mentors and networking are discussed in Chapter 6.

Flattery can be useful if it's not overdone or too obvious. Sometimes making a point of discussing progress and asking advice on your assignments, particularly the ones the boss is especially interested in, is helpful. Occasionally asking personal advice on your hopes and ambitions (if he's not later going to find you ignoring his advice) can be beneficial. The boss should know you're interested in getting ahead. However, don't emphasize hopes of advancing to echelons higher than his. Pointing out that you're planning to be a "competitor" for a better job than he has, president of the company for example, is not wise.

One form of flattery is participation in the same hobbies as the boss or in the same organizations. When a vice president of finance of a firm is a member of the Financial Executives Institute it has been noted that commonly the controller and treasurer who report to him also are members.

Sometimes an older male executive will regard a woman subordinate manager as a kind of "daughter" in terms of supplying advice and knowledge. She may resent it, but the woman may turn this to her advantage if, for instance, this provides her with considerable information on company politics.

5. Develop an "intelligence" system, grapevine contacts, to learn when opportunities for promotion may be coming up. This may include your boss, mentors, other influentials (or their staffs) within the company, or members of networks. An "intelligence" system is helpful in keeping you aware of what's going on. That can be important to you in your work and in providing clues to political situations that concern you in your company.

6. When a promotion opportunity comes up, or when you've done something important extraordinarily well, or when other circumstances make the timing right, ask for a promotion and/or a salary increase. Be careful, though, about accepting too small an advancement in position or salary when tactful insistence, or even waiting a bit, is likely to get you something bigger. A small bird in the hand may be worth a bigger one in the bush, but not if the bird in the bush has a high probability of soon landing in your hand.

7. Take the boss' suggestions seriously. Elizabeth Allen, merchandising vice president for a chain of women's apparel stores, reported to John Mueller, the president. Mueller knew, though others in the organization did not, that he was going to take early retirement in another 2 years. He considered recommending to his board of directors when the time came that Allen take his place. She had a college degree, but was lacking more than an elementary knowledge of accounting and finance. Mueller felt that a more advanced understanding of those functions in the business was important. One day he suggested to Allen, perhaps too casually, that she consider taking some evening courses in those subject areas at the local university. Her travel requirements might interfere occasionally with classes, but this need not be serious. Allen failed to take the hint. She did not enroll for the classes. Mueller never mentioned it again. On retiring he recommended somebody else for his replacement, and the board approved his selection. He confided to a consultant that the fact that his vice president had failed to recognize the importance of the financial area to the company, and had not taken his advice, really had bothered him.

8. Support your boss if you want him to support you. "Loyalty" is vital. This has already been touched on in discussing aggressiveness. At a sales meeting attended both by her boss, the sales vice president, and his boss, the company's president, Joan, a district sales manager, complained loudly that competition had a much better-looking package for its line of a food product than her own company. Her company's package was old-fashioned. It badly needed redesigning. If Joan had first quietly checked around she would have learned that her boss had only recently turned down, with the president's agreement, suggestions of redesign raised by the boss' headquarters staff. Had Joan then still strongly objected to the existing package she could have discussed her views with her boss privately, not in an open meeting, particularly one at which the boss' boss was also present. Joan was a very able district sales manager, but she waited a long time after that for a promotion to a larger district, and not because she was a woman. "Disloyalty," even in ignorance, is not easily forgiven.

9. Being politically attuned commonly means doing what is expedient, not what you believe is the right thing to do. Morality is not under discussion here, but rather the facts of organizational life. This means that if a woman has to choose sides she will want to be on the winning side in a critical power struggle within her organization, even though she prefers the losing side. It means if she doesn't agree with a proposed company policy, she won't fight it if that will win her influential enemies and but few friends in the organization. It means that if the company asks her to sell a product she knows is defective, she will have to sell it if she wants to get ahead in the company.

10. Try to avoid making enemies in the organization. This has been touched upon in discussing arrogance. Even noninfluential enemies may some day become influential. And try to avoid "slamming the door" on those with whom you've had a difference. Leave the door open a crack, just in case. Former enemies may later become allies, as well as vice versa.

11. One good turn begets another. John Jones, executive vice president of a publishing company, was joined by Jane Trevor, vice president of personnel, in a conspiracy. The objective was to

discredit the current president with his board of directors. They succeeded; the president resigned. The executive vice president was named president. Guess who became the first woman executive vice president the firm ever had? Jane Trevor, of course!

12. Recognize a good turn when you see it—and appreciate it. You may not get another from the same source. A firm's vice president of marketing scheduled a meeting with the president for a Saturday morning to talk about a facility expansion for product Y. He suggested to his staff assistant who had put together the pertinent figures that she come along. She had planned a birthday party for her eight year old daughter that Saturday morning. She could have begged off. Her boss didn't really need her at the meeting. However, she knew the exposure gained, a meeting and discussion with the president, could only be helpful to her future in the company. She went. Some months later a vacancy arose in another department. The president thought of her, spoke to her boss, and she was transferred to a new job that constituted a considerable promotion.

13. Recognize an opportunity to do a good turn where it counts. Paula was risk manager for her company. That meant she handled the purchase of the company's insurance needs. The company had been buying a good part of its insurance through the Jonathan Insurance Agency. One day Paula learned by chance from an outside source that the president's son-in-law had gone into the insurance business with the Marathon Insurance Agency. Paula investigated, found Marathon could at similar cost provide insurance policies equivalent to those now bought through Jonathan. She checked through her boss to make sure there would be no objection to a switch. She wanted to be sure the president wasn't "mad" at his son-in-law, that the head of Jonathan wasn't the president's best friend, and that the president would not object to an appearance of undue nepotism (the president could honestly claim he had not himself initiated a switch in the placement of the company's insurance). She was reassured. The insurance business was then switched to Marathon, of course for some very rational business reasons. Paula's political initiative later paid off for her.

Wherever large numbers of people are working together in a

group for common goals, as in a corporation, and wherever there is an interplay of rivalries for position and power, you will find politics involved. You may have more of it in one company than in another, but you have it, to one degree or another, in all companies. It's a fact of life.

4

Dealing with Peers, Bosses, and Spouses

Competition

The woman who wants to get ahead in her organization faces widespread resentment from the men she works with, because she is a woman. This is especially the case where women have taken over jobs that were formerly the exclusive province of the male. Resentment tends to diminish with time, yet an undercurrent of animosity is likely to continue to exist.

That men perceive in the peer woman a competitor and a threat is illustrated by the comment of a Chicago purchasing executive, a man, who refers to "men's lack of security with respect to their own abilities and performance" as an obstacle to a woman's progress in his company. A young San Francisco professional explains that the men she works with "often feel threatened by my competence (. . . sometimes I have felt I had to downplay it to be effective)." A similar thought is expressed by the female vice president of marketing of a New York firm: "Learning not to threaten by excellence because you're already 'different.' "

A travel industry executive in New York expresses her belief that it is especially the older man who looks upon the woman as an unwanted competitor: "It is an older (fifty years) less technically qualified person [man] in a 'peer' position through 'tenure' who may feel particularly threatened."

Sometimes it is the younger man who still has his future ahead of him who more keenly feels the competition. The older man at least has already been promoted to about as far as he would go anyway and he has seniority to protect tenure.

A few years ago one of our larger public utilities under government prodding, began to newly open up middle management positions to women, formerly excluded. The men had been under the impression that the path of their upward mobility lay clear and unobstructed before them. Now they saw that path blocked. They perceived a preempting of their own future advancement by women who would be moved in to fill goals dictated by "affirmative action." Women would now be favored, just because they were women. The male bitterness was considerable.

Alma Baron, University of Wisconsin management professor, found that 56 percent of over 8,000 male managers surveyed felt threatened by women whom they believed would be promoted faster than themselves.[7]

In another survey, one of 602 officers (only 8 were women) of large U.S. companies, conducted by Louis Harris & Associates, Inc., for *Business Week,* 8 percent agreed that "some men now can't get ahead in certain jobs because they are being saved for women." The 8 percent as a general figure for managers is believed to be low, since "the executives surveyed are so high on the corporate ladder (about two-thirds are chief executive officers) that they themselves are not professionally threatened by competition from women executives."[8]

Most of both the male and female executives I surveyed believe men strongly resent promotions of women which otherwise would have gone to men. Resentment surfaces in and is reinforced by the peer male's tendency to look upon the woman associate in his firm not as an equal, but as an "equal, *but.*" A major portion of both men and women queried believe this attitude exists. Only a little over one-third of the women questioned, and half of the men, claim that in their companies peer males consider women colleagues to be really their equals. About a fourth of both men and of women think the male perceives the female associate to be unduly favored because she is a woman, someone who has to be tolerated, an unwanted competitor. A few of the men and women surveyed believe peer males consider the woman to be downright inferior.

What can the woman do about the resentment towards females? Aside from the possible help of a couple of male mentors, particularly powerful ones (see Chapter 6), meet it directly at times on a confrontational basis? Maybe! But it's probably more productive in most cases for her to gain the respect of the men she works with through the quality of her work, working harder and better; and at the same time trying to "fit in" and to get along with the men. A bit of tact in not too aggressively, too suddenly, too openly threatening the male with her excellence, while not overly downplaying her competence either, should be useful. A bit of humor in handling sensitive situations should also help.

That's how Marge Woller, lone woman in a headquarters group of a dozen males in a fair-sized chemical company, handled it. Marge and the men were all chemists or chemical engineers, all competent. But there *was* resentment when a woman first joined the group. It took a while, but with time, through the quality of her work, a "controlled" aggressiveness that strengthened gradually, not too suddenly, a tactful "fitting in," and a successful effort slowly to push her way into full membership in informal luncheon get-togethers and after-hours Friday sessions at the local "watering hole" (bar)—resentment died down and acceptance took its place.

A warning is volunteered by a number of the male executives surveyed. Trying too hard to "fit in" by emulating the men in terms of "male characteristics"—roughness of language, over-aggressiveness—may be counter-productive.

A principle of "controlled patience" may be relevant. Expect resentment and don't expect it to disappear too quickly. Time is required for the male, through familiarity and necessity, to "rationalize" away initial resentment.

It's interesting to note the view of Margaret Hennig and Anne Jardim on resentment, and acceptance, as expressed in their book, *The Managerial Woman*. They examine in some detail the careers of 25 women who have held top management positions in business and industry. The authors refer to the women's assumed acceptance of themselves by the men they dealt with. The group abstained from negative assumptions of rejection which women with self-doubts about their ability to fill a job sometimes telegraph to their male associates. Those self-doubts reinforce male doubts about whether the women belong in their jobs, and with it, male resentment. Quoting from the authors: ". . . they *expected* positive reactions and acted as if they did until they were proven wrong. . . . their implicit assumption of acceptance rather than of rejection allowed them to deal with men at every hierarchical level in a way which compelled those who felt negatively about them to act first—to raise the issue in a vacuum as a consequence of the individual man's personal difficulties rather than as a consequence of the individual woman's signal that she *expected* negative reactions."[9]

"Affirmative Action"

How strong a factor has government requirements for "affirmative action" to overcome discrimination been? Of the organization women surveyed, only 21 percent directly credit affirmative action for expediting promotion to their present jobs. Many others prefer to attribute promotions to their abilities rather than quotas. But it can well be argued that without the crowbar of quotas, the abilities may not have been enough.

Affirmative action, because it has opened doors for organization women, has also caused resentment. The vice president of a Minneapolis concern complains about "having a woman placed in a technical position based on a need for affirmative action commitment goal vs. being the most qualified person available."

Interestingly, a woman executive in Texas points out "being promoted in competition with a male—difficult; being hired into a highly paid position in competition—easy." A woman hired into a position from the outside fulfills affirmative action quotas. A woman promoted internally instead of a man can cause greater resentment than the outsider. The same Texas executive claims that in "my experience the male peer desires to be fair and free of bias; however, he is deeply influenced through male peer pressure and at the same time fears female competition."

Despite affirmative action, discrimination still exists. Women in most cases still have to be harder working and brighter than their male counterparts to achieve a given job level. Of the male executives queried, 44 percent feel that the managerial and professional woman, despite resentment towards her, is likely to be looked upon by the men in her peer group as someone to be respected for her abilities. Of the career women themselves, 60 percent feel that "to a significant degree I am looked upon by men in my peer group as someone to be respected for my abilities."

Spouse Pressure

The greatest foe of the woman who wants to get ahead in her organization may well be not the male, but the male's spouse, her peer's wife or her boss' wife. To that wife the career woman represents in a sense either a kind of competitor or an object of envy. (See Kanter's discussion of the concern of wives about the potential for sex in the working relationships between husbands and their female peers.[10]) Over three-fourths of the women and two-thirds of the male executives questioned believe men's wives resent considerably after-hours or out-of-town meetings which include both their husbands and career women. The organization woman's husband also is likely to resent those same meetings. Most of the organization women and almost half of the men believe wives resent not only the meetings, but the career women generally. So, if you weren't invited to accompany the men to that trade convention in Miami or New York or Las Vegas; or if you don't get that promotion, or that raise you thought you deserved and were sure to get—it's possible the other woman, the wife, is responsible.

How to win wives over? Don't dress seductively for company social affairs or meetings where they are to be present. In conversing with peer wives personally or on the telephone, treat them as your equals. Don't be condescending if they're stay-at-homes. Avoid giving any impression that relationships at the office are more than strictly business.

A *Wall Street Journal* article quotes one woman as suggesting: "Talk to spouses. Don't wait for them to take the initiative." The same article also points out that the wife of a male subordinate can present a problem. "To prove her disinterest, one single woman boss took her male employee and his jealous wife to dinner, 'and I made sure I had a date.' "[11]

Women on Women

The upwardly mobile career woman is resented not only by male peers and their spouses. Her female peers in the organization, and of course females in the lower ranks, also resent her. Women don't have to be wives to resent other women. By more than three to one, career women who are bosses themselves prefer a male to a female boss.

The senior vice-president of a Virginia bank comments on "the petty jealousies among peers due to lack of self-confidence and self-esteem." A Dallas respondent charges that "women tend to act like barracudas towards each other—the more responsible the position, the more so." A Houston district manager complains of a "desire to outshine each other; lack of trust; lack of willingness to share (i.e., experiences, information, etc.)." And a San Francisco manager notes that because of distrust and rivalry it's hard to make friends with other women in her organization.

Organization women were asked what they considered to be the most difficult, irritating, frustrating, and/or distasteful problem(s) for them as women in working with *other women*. Fully a third volunteered comments falling into the category: "Their resentment, lack of support, competitiveness, distrust." Male executives also refer frequently to this resentment and lack of support for each other among women. For the woman who wants to get ahead in her organization this lack of mutual support, the reluctance to share knowledge and experience on problems encountered, doesn't help. The competitiveness is understandable in light of the few managerial jobs and promotions available to women relative to the many who would like to have them. The intensity of the rivalry is likely to diminish as the number of positions open to women increases.

What can be done? A special effort to be friendly may be beneficial. Care to avoid aggravating sensitive situations or feelings is worthwhile. Working together over time may help mutual understanding. Minimize the fact that you may be competitors.

Male Chauvinism

One of the most difficult problems faced by the organization woman in working with *men* is "unequal treatment" as compared with the man—male chauvinism. Over half of the women queried volunteered comments falling into this category. Certainly chauvinism, and the discrimination that is part of it, constitutes the single most difficult sex-related obstacle career women face in getting ahead. Some quotations from males may be pertinent.

A Los Angeles department manager indicates that "a strong obstacle to a woman's getting ahead in my company is the negative attitude toward females in the work force; the attitude of upper management [in refusing] . . . to accept women in their ranks, to see their potential, and provide appropriate exposure to a diverse part of the organization." An Indianapolis executive refers to the difficulties faced by career women in his firm because of " 'old-style' managers who have been around a long time, generally males from the old school when women belonged at home. We still have plenty of these in upper management levels."

Critical remarks such as these by males are most likely to be made by younger rather than older executives, at least by those younger men who don't feel personally threatened by female competition. It is the older men, though not exclusively so, who are particularly chauvinistic.

And note that the senior executives in an organization, the top bosses, are generally older men. It takes time to climb the corporate ladder. The top jobs in an organization will therefore for the most part be filled by older men, especially in mature industries and established firms. It is then the older men, the top bosses, who set policy on promotions, particularly in the higher positions. This makes it tough, but with time and the help of affirmative action, the situation for the organization woman should improve.

The presence of male chauvinism is most keenly felt, of course, by the career woman who suffers from it. Thus an older woman in San Francisco is troubled by her firm's "management attitudes towards women. The company does not project an image of doing what's right, equitable, but what's required by law and no more" in being fair to the women in its employ. And despite her own personal success, the vice president of a Colorado bank, laments "a generation of men (over forty-five to fifty) who still view women with uncertainty."

Interestingly, on the other side of the coin is the complaint of a young male executive in San Francisco about the women he deals with in his firm—"their tendency to believe that every new male they come into contact with is a chauvinist. Guilty until proven innocent."

Chauvinism within an organization may be aggravated by the chauvinism of outsiders with whom the organization must deal. Thus the executive vice president of a New York advertising agency, a highly successful woman in her forties, complains of the difficulties encountered in "getting clients to accept a woman in a management role." Such acceptance is obviously fundamental to the acceptance of a woman within the agency itself.

Career women tend to find particularly aggravating the male habit of "not giving full recognition to me—deferring to a man if a question needs answering." A related complaint is voiced by a female vice president: "Being talked down to and not being given an opportunity to comment . . . "

Another irritation among women is the necessity cited by a woman engineer with one of the major defense contractors for continually "having to re-establish my 'credentials' every time there is a new group [of men] with which to deal. Assumption I'm a secretary." That image, the preconception that the woman is a secretary, sets up a hurdle in establishing an appropriate framework for professional and managerial relationships with her male counterparts.

Michael G. Zey in *The Mentor Connection* postulates: "Since female managers are intentionally and unintentionally confused with women of lower status, many react by avoiding contact with such women. Perhaps because most nonprofessional office personnel, especially clerical workers and secretaries, are women, the female manager has countered such misidentification by disassociating herself from most other corporate females: she attempts to dress 'professionally'; she assumes the characteristics and mannerisms of the managerial class; and above all she tries to be seen in the company of men."[12]

Prejudice and sex discrimination in hiring, in pay for similar jobs, and in promotion is still rampant. It's just less often openly practiced and admitted than formerly.

Discrimination starts with the failure even to admit women to certain types of jobs and to positions in higher management. A St. Louis personnel manager, a woman, explains that in her corporation "men still think of 'men's' jobs and 'women's' jobs. They tend to generalize too often" in this way. An assistant marketing manager in California expresses her frustration with the complaint that "there are less than 10 percent of women who work [in nonclerical and nonsecretarial level jobs in her firm] . . . what has always been a *male* heavy industry; difficult-to-crack political infrastructure." And "accepting a woman in the forging business" has been tough for an older woman in a town in northern Illinois.

Writing in the *American Economic Review* for May 1976, on "The Economic Status of Women in the United States," M. D. Keyserling points out: "Yet according to recent statistics, 75 percent of them are concentrated in the five predominantly 'female professions': secretary-stenographer, household worker, bookkeeper, elementary school teacher and waitress."

The concentration of women in "women's" jobs still holds to a large degree. Government estimates for 1982 show the following numbers of females in the job categories given (numbers are in millions):[13]

Clerks and kindred workers (the majority—secretaries, typists, bookkeepers, cashiers, and office machine operators)	14.89
Food service workers (two thirds of them waitresses and cooks)	3.13
Sales workers	2.99
Teachers (including college and university)	2.52
Health service workers (chiefly nursing aides and practical nurses)	1.81
Registered nurses, dieticians and therapists	1.59
Personal service workers	1.42
Private household workers	1.01

The total, 29.4 million, constitutes 68% of the females employed in 1982.

A senior corporate public affairs specialist points out that in her organization "women are in middle management, but still not considered for line management positions. Good staff jobs, but . . ."

Even in liberated companies, as an Oregon woman executive expresses it, "there may be a feeling that one or two women [in higher echelons and in line positions] are OK, but more, undesirable."

By one estimate women comprise 8 percent of middle managers and 2.5 percent of senior managers.[14] The figure of 2.5 percent is high for the really top jobs.

A woman's progress in her company is impeded by the "old boy" networks through which much hiring and promotion into the better jobs occur, and of which women are *not* generally a part.

The discomfort of a male executive in dealing with women on a peer basis sets up a further barrier. A New York executive cites his "own relative inexperience. I had three brothers, no sisters. I feel more at ease and more patient with men." A female senior vice president in St. Louis points out that in her organization "because women executives are currently a minority, certain male executives may be uncomfortable with directly interacting with a woman with regularity."

A Chicago investment officer points to the male breadwinner syndrome that still exists in some places. As she explains, "men find it difficult to promote a woman with the same qualifications (or better) over a man—because he supports family.''

Pay and Promotion

The majority of career women believe their companies do not pay them as well as they pay men in similar jobs and at similar responsibility levels. Few believe they are better paid.

The following, from an older career woman in a mid-size Eastern city, illustrates one facet of pay discrimination. " . . . right now I find discrimination on the basis of my sex to be the hardest factor to deal with. I am the only woman in the company where I work. The work itself is quite specialized . . . However, the men here do not recognize the fact that should I leave, not one of them could come in to take over my job, even if I became ill and was out of work for several days [only]. They grant themselves huge raises every year and I am treated almost with disdain. The statement has been made to me that 'You make a good salary here in . . . , for a woman.' "

A San Francisco woman comments: "There are . . . women [specialists] in a department of . . . [over 100]. All are paid less than the comparable men, according to our secret information from the computer."

The following statement by an older buying executive, a female, bears on another aspect of compensation discrimination, at least as she perceives it: "I control about . . . million dollars in cars and trucks as I am a fleet administrator along with my purchasing chores. Although I am called upon every day to give advice on . . . [very large and expensive] . . . trucks, etc., my company does not see fit to include any women in key positions in their stock option plan or bonus plan.

"This irritates me considerably but I am at an age where there isn't much I can do about it. Hopefully, when I retire I am going to have my say and perhaps help others."

Most women feel that in their firm the likelihood of getting promoted is less for a woman than for a man, given equal qualifications and experience. The odds against the woman's being promoted to a job increases with the pay for that job. Male executives too feel that a woman is discriminated against in promotions, at least for the better-paying jobs.

A couple of female comments on promotions for women are perceptive. From a San Francisco research engineer: "Because there are so few women, everything that we do stands out. Good job performance tends to be overshadowed by bad performance." From a Richmond, Virginia, bank officer: "Tendency of males to be overly protective and hesitant about putting her in a position that may result in failure. Males are [promoted and thus] permitted to succeed or fail."

Further Aspects

Discrimination is found in the unequal treatment of women in other than hiring, pay, and promotion. For example, it is to be found in the assignment of work within a group. The more menial, routine, less challenging and potentially less rewarding tasks, uninspiring detail and "grunt" work are more likely to go to the women in a group of professionals or managers than to their male peers. Thus a female officer in the marketing department of a Missouri bank finds it irritating that "you're usually asked to do the minor details on any project." A Houston accounting manager, referring to her experience, finds a "tendency to assign the more secretarial types of administrative duties to women."

A department manager in a northeastern Pennsylvania city complains that "men can leave the office at any time for coffee, errands, etc., where most all women [including herself] are expected to be at their desk 9 to 5."

Unequal treatment is found in the greater respect accorded by women themselves to men than to women in comparable management positions. A northern California insurance manager charges: "I am the only woman executive . . . I share a secretarial pool with . . . men executives and my work is always done last, if at all."

Reference to respect brings up another item. At company meetings, social affairs, and conventions which include both career men and career women, profanity, drinking, and telling dirty stories are common. There is considerable participation by the women—31 percent of the females join in profanity; almost three-fourths join in drinking; 11 percent sometimes and another 1 percent frequently join in the telling of raunchy stories. The participation may be voluntary and a sign of increasing equality of the sexes. For some women, however, it may represent compulsion to conform, a kind of harassment. And harassment, sexual and otherwise, does exist, widely. Sexual overtones including harassment are discussed in Chapter 11.

There's another form of unequal treatment which has been mentioned by some of the career women queried. This is chivalry. The women perceive it to be a form of condescension: put-downs, perhaps unconscious; a throwback to the period when women were supposed to be accepting of second-class citizenship. Thus a San Francisco manager, a divorcee in her thirties supervising mostly men, is irked by "chivalry—especially the 'showy' kind;" and a Portland, Oregon accounting supervisor complains of "the overprotective male who almost knocks me down to open a door or pull out a chair."

Other career women don't appreciate men who "try to be so helpful. Too accommodating;" or the "overly protective male chauvinist."

Veering to a slightly different aversion is a bank vice president in the Northwest, a married woman in her forties, who objects to "older men [who] tend to want to 'godfather' you and provide 'gifts' of jobs and promotions. Young men wish you weren't around at all."

Some males, like an older man, a vice president of human resources in New Jersey, find it difficult even with good intentions to treat a woman "as equal rather than 'as a lady' as I was brought up [to do]."

An exploration of male chauvinism and discrimination faced by the career woman must include reference to a common tactic employed by the male against the woman, exclusion. This is found in the exclusion of the woman from informal all-male decision-making meetings of her peers—sometimes deliberately staged in the men's washroom—that affect her work; exclusion from or delayed transmission of information important to her work; and exclusion from all-male clubs where men entertain and conduct business. There is some, but apparently a limited tendency to exclusion of women from lunch or other on-the-job socializing with male colleagues. Off-the-job socializing is less frequent, two-thirds of the career women surveyed claiming "not much" such socializing.

The female vice president of a large New York company is excluded from decision making by reason of "their [men] holding ad hoc meetings in the bathroom." A Chicago woman describes her situation: "I am part of the team—right up to the moment of decision making—then the 'team' suddenly becomes all male." Another woman, a New York vice president, complains about "not being able to gain entry to meetings held in exclusively male clubs (happens infrequently, but occasionally)." What the manager of worldwide sales operations for a large company finds "most difficult is not totally being made aware of meetings which take place at corporate levels and decisions made which affect indirectly my operations."

A Detroit vice president, a man, indicates "there tends to be male dominated social/business related activities (golf outings, cards, after-work drinks) that make it hard for a woman to become totally accepted;" and this is confirmed by the woman executive vice president of a New York corporation who complains of the "lack of acceptance on the social (golf, evening events, etc.) level."

A similar problem tends to arise in respect to after-hours drinking at the local "watering hole"—the bar to which men may repair after work. At the routine (at least on Fridays) "happy hour" a lot of information is swapped and vital contacts established, but chiefly when it's all "the boys." A woman may not be unwelcome, but it's on the old "Ah, things are shaping up around here!" basis of "come-on"—business goes down the tubes ("We're boring Margie.").

This is understandable. Kanter points out that management structure and communication is such as to encourage exclusion of those people (women) with whom managers (men) feel uncomfortable, because they (women) are somehow "different." [15]

What can women do to counter the exclusion, aside from not of their own accord excluding themselves by not being available, particularly for after-hours activities? If golf is the favored activity in the male management group, presumably the woman might learn to play golf. But whether or not she plays golf, proving herself congenial and relaxing company, with worthwhile thoughts to contribute, bright questions to ask—enjoyable to be with on a colleague or buddy—but not on a sexual—basis, should be helpful. Of course this is sometimes easier said than done. And children, even a husband, can get in the way of after-hours or weekend sociability with the "boys". The resentment of the wives of the "boys," another problem too, in respect to management women joining in social activities with the peer husbands, has been referred to earlier.

Men discriminate; and don't like women to complain about it. This is evident in the sensitivity of male executives to women who raise questions concerning discrimination, "imagined" or real. The senior vice president of a Boston corporation finds irritating the "over-assertion of women's rights and claims of current discrimination." An Oakland, California, controller objects to the woman "who is immature and over-emotional—who sees sex discrimination behind every reprimand or other setback." And another male comments: "A woman's sensitivity to being a woman. Many are so concerned about being discriminated against they perceive attitudes which are not true."

A vice president of manufacturing is frustrated in "dealing with those women that cannot see a difference between sexual discrimination and organizational politics. No one can be exempt from the latter." A North Carolina executive claims "when things don't go their way, some of them blame it on prejudice." And a Massachusetts corporate vice president finds it most difficult to deal with women, particularly those paranoid on the subject, "trying to push as the 'liberator.' "

Fully 12 percent of the men surveyed refer in their volunteered comments to women's oversensitivity to discrimination against women, some "imagined," and who "push too hard" for women's rights.

Even an occasional woman gets irritated with women "attributing lack of success to the fact that they are female rather than making a serious effort to overcome shortcomings"—this from a female director of customer activities.

What's the answer to chauvinism and discrimination? Confrontation in the more blatant cases—with a touch of diplomacy? The woman facing a male peer or boss who fancies himself sympathetic to the progress of women may be able to get somewhere in confrontation. If he is civilized enough to feel guilt, she has leverage. Or if a company is under legal pressure on the score of sex discrimination, there's a chance to make gains.

On the other hand, if old attitudes are strong with the male hierarchy, appealing to "fairness" doctrine or to nonexistent guilt requires "whistle-blowing" legal recourse to get results. However, the organization woman should be prepared then to terminate her career, certainly career progress, with her present employer, and quite possibly with some other prospective employers. Other recourses? Performance—most of all; gentle persuasion, over time—possibly; hope for a change in management or attitude at the top, which will filter down to the level of her boss or peer—conceivably; or a change in employment.

Where the boss is obdurately chauvinistic, but the boss' boss or top management in an organization is not, there may be a chance to appeal over the immediate boss' head on the more extreme cases of discrimination. But the man for whom the woman is now working won't appreciate her appeal, and won't forget it. One has to be prepared to get a transfer to another boss in the organization. See Chapter 12 on a woman's legal rights.

5

Dealing with Subordinates

Woman Boss and Male Subordinate

One of the key abilities an ambitious woman must possess is to motivate the people who work for her. But in the view of a goodly share of top corporate management in the U.S., women on the whole are less able than men to motivate their subordinates, male or female. Though there are exceptions, the discomfort in having a woman for a boss is strong, especially for the male. For a man to have a female superior is not at all consistent with the traditional male image. As a woman marketing manager comments: "Many [men] resent even the slightest directives from women." And in the words of another woman manager, men find it difficult "accepting the fact that I am in charge. That I can kick, and fire—just taking instruction from a woman [is hard for a male to swallow]." The situation is especially aggravated when the job experience of a subordinate male exceeds that of the woman boss, as sometimes happens.

The circumstance of a male reporting to a woman can be

aggravating to the woman too. One female boss describes her irritation in having "to instruct a new insecure arrogant young man who 'knows everything' and I have to let him learn by trial and error because he refuses to accept proven procedures, generally because of (1) trying to create an impression and (2) male chauvinism. Generally this is short-lived." Another boss lady refers to "working through the ego problems many men seem to have when they first report to me, especially men my own age or older."

A man may resent a woman boss because he thinks that working for a female will hurt his career. The most influential managers, and therefore those who may be most helpful in getting subordinates like himself promoted, are perceived to be men.

The male executive is well aware of the male subordinate's sensitivity. It is definitely an inhibiting factor in the promotion of women. As a female manager explains, a woman may not be promoted because "this will mean more males reporting to her."

Top management is not anxious to promote rebellion in their ranks by placing women in command positions over men. Being men themselves they appreciate and empathize with the view of the male who does not like reporting to a woman. This is partly why "boss ladies" far more often boss other women than they do men.

Women and Women Bosses

Women too resent boss ladies, and male executives are aware of this. The senior vice president of a large Oregon firm is only one of a group of male executives who note that women "sometimes seem to have difficulty managing other women." There is indeed a very strong preference, something over three to one, by the career women surveyed, for a male rather than a female boss. Kanter[17] discusses at some length the hypothesis that a preference (by both men and women) for male bosses reflects the desire the subordinates have for working under bosses that have power. Male bosses are perceived to have more power, generally, than do women bosses.

One woman executive complains that "most women still stereotype women 'bosses' as more demanding, not as competent, etc.'' Some of the resentment of female subordinates for female bosses is unquestionably related to envy and jealousy. A woman may have learned to accept male dominance. She's been taught it all her life. But dominance by her own sex? That's something else!

Perhaps too, a feeling of insecurity on the part of the lady boss, overcompensated by a fear of admitting ever to be wrong in dealing with other women, is a factor in the resentment of female subordinates. A Flushing, New York career women reports that ''my experience with a woman supervisor was that she was continually right and would never accept new ideas.''

Observations from the boss ladies include a marked ''initial discomfort at having a woman boss, especially for the first time.'' ''Some do not want to take orders from me.'' ''As a young woman I often have trouble not being respected by older women subordinates.'' ''Unwanted familiarity.'' ''Subordinate women *expect* 'favors' from women that they would not even *ask* men for.'' ''Resented—not recognized as a woman department manager—not given the same treatment as male counterparts.'' ''Their prejudice at my success, i.e., jealousy.'' ''Resentment of my position at a fairly young age.''

Older subordinate women without advanced education are particularly prone to ''resent young career women with college education'' [to whom they report].

One also encounters, much less frequently, a touch of hero worship by subordinate females of their female superiors. Two comments: ''Expectations that I must be able to 'walk on water;' '' and ''Pedestalizing.''

Resentment of a woman boss can be overcome. This takes a style of management that minimizes rather than encourages resentment. Indeed, women's ascribed lesser ability to motivate may in part be tied to style of management.

Women appear to be more authoritarian and ''demanding'' than men, at least of women. Both the men and the women surveyed believe this; and subordinates resent it. Of the women expressing themselves, 76 percent are themselves bosses.

That women bosses may be more demanding (than men), at least of women subordinates, is not surprising. Women may understand other women better than do men, and a boss lady may therefore hesitate less to demand output from another woman. A man may not recognize a woman's below-par performance to be mere malingering as quickly as will a female. He may also be more reluctant to crack down on women. Shades of "chivalry"? A woman may also figure that since she worked hard getting up the corporate ladder, as a woman, other women can work just as hard.

The female treasurer of a Nevada transportation firm, in her early thirties, relates that "most of my own experience with older women managers was not good for me. They had it rough climbing up the promotional ladder, so they made it difficult for any women working under them." Another woman comments that women bosses "seem too domineering and wanting to be 'bossy' over other women." A female analyst in Memphis complains of "encounters with stereotypical 'managerial bitches.' " The point seemingly is confirmed by the operations vice president of a Minneapolis manufacturer, an older woman, who explains: "My expectations are for them [women subordinates] to perform and work like I did . . ."

Styles of Management

A demanding style of management, such as many women apparently have, a style that is essentially authoritarian, dictatorial, in its viewpoint of how people should be bossed is commonly called Theory X management. It is often not the most productive style. On the other hand, management that believes subordinates should be encouraged to take part in discussing the objectives and the how and why of what they do at work is called Theory Y management. A woman manager remains the boss with Theory Y, but she assumes subordinates have at least some brains, some capacity and desire to do a good job, and some ability to contribute out of their own experience and knowledge and intelligence to furthering the work objectives of the group of which they are a part. In other words, an X manager tells the subordinate what to do and how to do it, and asks no advice from the individual who is going to do it. The Y manager tells the subordinate what to do, but not always how to do it. In any case, Y encourages the individual who is going to do the work to think about it, to offer suggestions, to participate in figuring out how best to get a job done.

Participative Y-type management is more productive than the authoritarian X-type where subordinates need to use some thought in their work. X-type is likely to be more productive where heavy manual work, disagreeable work, or mind-numbing routine requiring little independent thought is involved. With both types of management, and all those in-betweens which constitute most management, rationality and competency are obviously necessary, and fairness is important.

Good morale and the efficient operation of a group require that its manager, and especially a woman manager, be considered to be rational and competent. It is equally important that the woman manager be fair, and be *perceived* to be fair, to subordinates in what she expects in work output and quality; how she allocates the work to be done; how she evaluates; and how she disciplines. Being fair is fundamental to being respected (as differentiated from being feared). Being fair means avoiding either favoring or disfavoring particular individuals among subordinates or one sex versus the other.

Survey figures are not conclusive, but point to provocative possibilities. The top management men queried may feel, just a little, that female bosses are fairer than male bosses in dealing with their subordinates. A bit inconsistently, however, they seem to feel women managers more than men play favorites with particular individuals, and slightly favor men as a group over women. The men seem also to feel that women tend to seek advice and opinions from subordinates more than do men; and that women claim less credit to themselves than do men for the ideas and the work of subordinates. Giving credit, and promptly, where credit is due, is a great morale booster and loyalty builder. Withholding credit, and even worse, stealing it, is destructive of morale and loyalty.

The dislike for a woman boss is less than it used to be. This is particularly true for the younger men, as well as the younger women who have entered the job market in recent years. The woman's movement and affirmative action have expedited changes in attitudes. The availability of more and better qualified female candidates for managerial and professional jobs with the increasing numbers of young women receiving a management or professional education, and subsequent training, have further helped. Dislike of the female-in-charge can be expected to continue to diminish. As the number and experience of women bosses increase, as they will, subordinate males and females will become more accustomed to the presence of the female manager, a qualified and confident one. With familiarity will come acceptance.

In the larger organizations where affirmative action has been taken seriously and women managers are no longer a rarity, a self-confident woman who is a good manager is still likely to find undertones of gender resentment, but in most cases nothing that she cannot handle. She does have to be a good manager, but so does a man. If she is able and firm and fair to both sexes, in time she'll be accepted by both men and women subordinates.

Infrequently a woman manager may run into one or more incorrigible males, subordinates who refuse to heed orders, continually ignore them, and insist on doing things in their own way. An open discussion of the problem often helps. If not, it may be necessary to resort to an old method of enforcing discipline, the threat of firing, or an actual discharge, perhaps of only the worst offender—as an example. Transfer of offenders to another department and another boss is a less drastic alternative.

The part played by style of management in motivating subordinates has been referred to. Aside from style, what are some of the motivators which the woman manager should keep in mind?

Monetary rewards can be used where the manager is empowered to provide them. The ability to adjust salaries for performance is likely to be limited, however, by an organization's standardized pay scales, what other segments of the organization pay for similar work, and what union-management negotiations produce. Merit raises can be given subordinates, within the limits permitted by organizational rules and one's budget. Once a salary raise is given, however, it becomes accepted as an expected right and tends to lose its ability to motivate. There is of course the hope, the carrot, of further increases in remuneration, but again restricted, except as salary can be considerably increased if there is a promotion. But the number of promotions to be parcelled out is limited, and are likely to be given to those who are star performers, strivers, self-driven to perform in any case.

A commission system of pay and bonuses to individuals based on their performance can motivate. The means of evaluating performance must be accepted as reasonably valid and fair. Commissions, bonuses, and special prizes to competitive contest winners are often used in sales programs. They can be effective. A bonus based on what a group produces can serve to motivate where the performance measured is largely the result of team rather than individual effort.

Fringe benefits are for the most part standardized, but sometimes within budgetary limits a manager may be able to parcel out company-paid trips to conventions or trade shows as a reward for good performance. Again, these are likely to go to those who are motivated to perform well in any case.

Status symbols—title, an individuals's own enclosed office, pictures on the wall, furniture, the quality of the carpeting and drapes, etc. have been used to motivate. They're likely to do as much harm to the morale of those subordinates who don't get them as good in terms of increased performance from those who do.

Other nonmonetary recognition can be motivating to subordinates—an invitation to lunch or dinner with the boss to show appreciation for a particularly good performance, an employee-of-the-month award, or a certificate of merit presented in the presence of the subordinate's co-workers and perhaps higher-ups.

A reputation that a particular manager tries and is able to promote or place able subordinates in good jobs in her organization can be a motivator. A woman executive in a large manufacturing concern illustrates the point: "I have a reputation for going out of my way to seek out and get my people promoted to desirable spots in the company. People *want* to work for me."

Rotation among subordinates and enlargement of job duties can be helpful at times in getting the most out of subordinates where the work is repetitive, dull, and boring. So can structuring of jobs, where it is possible, to allow some room for creativity and its satisfactions.

Competition within or between groups of subordinates can sometimes be used without rewards of money or the equivalent. In some situations it can help make a boring job a little less boring. The initiation of quality control charts to improve quality by showing an employee group how it is doing, hourly or daily, on product defects or clerical errors works on a similar principle—competition, whether with other groups or its own past performance.

Occasionally competition backfires. Jane Dall was a research chemist with Company A. She was relatively happy. Through a friend she was offered a job for similar pay with Company B, working in the same field as with A. She jumped at the chance, for company B had a policy of paying a chemist a bonus based on a percentage of all royalties collected from the licensing of patents resulting from the work of that chemist. A number of B's chemists had become wealthy collecting on those royalties.

Two years later Jane asked for her old job back at Company A, and being known as an excellent chemist she got it. She had found at Company B that the desire for patents credit for new chemicals and processes, and the income from the patents, was so great that the chemists in B's laboratory individually kept to themselves the results of work done. Interchange of ideas and progress on research was minimized in a situation where the rate of innovation and invention inevitably depended on such interchange. And with the absence of communication came also a lack of the professional satisfactions arising from "consensual validation" by professional associates.

Similar divisiveness, a lack of candid intercommunication, is sometimes found among managers jockeying for political advantage within their organizations; and among women competing intensely with each other for what they perceive to be a limited number of the better jobs available to them in their companies.

It is of interest to note that whether for job security or other reasons people tend to work faster when they see a lot of work stacked up ahead, than when they can only see a limited amount of work to be done. In one large retail organization some time ago clerks, all female, would manually post daily to customer accounts entries of charge purchases made. These charges subsequently would be billed. The women at that time were paid on a piecework basis. The more postings a woman made in a given time, the greater was her pay. Yet despite the piecework pay system, the *hourly* output of postings per clerk, by the very same clerks, for purchases made in January, a relatively weak month for sales, was less than half the *hourly* output of posting per clerk for sales made in the busy Christmas month of December.

Maximizing the performance of subordinates is closely tied to treating people as people. Subordinates should feel they can readily and comfortably approach their manager for clarification, advice, and support in the execution of their job assignments, and in meeting work objectives.

Delegating

Delegating starts with breaking up the duties of a manager into a number of segments. These are defined in terms of the tasks to be performed for each. Task assignments are then matched to the group of people and the individuals who are to perform them. In matching, special skills for the different tasks have to be kept in mind. The workload delegated should be balanced insofar as possible, so that each group for its size and each individual has an equivalent workload. Where an imbalance exists reorganization of task assignments may be called for.

As workloads change, organizational shifts in assignments or changes in numbers of personnel needed will occur. The woman manager needs to be aware of altered requirements. She will need to adjust assignments of personnel and facilities accordingly. *Complete* workload equalization, of course, may not be possible.

A manager needs to explain carefully task assignments, and needs to be sure explanations are clearly understood by subordinates. The performance expected of subordinates should also be clearly understood. Standards for performance should be defined insofar as standards exist or can be set. Reports on performance and interim reports on uncompleted assignments should be called for as appropriate. The monitoring of performance and of progress on uncompleted assignments is part of the job of a manager. This may be through both formal and informal reports, written or oral. The manager may also use walk-throughs or field visits, personally viewing the work being done, talking to and asking questions of her subordinates, and of their subordinates too.

Monitoring can be overdone. Once a manager has assigned a task there should be no need continually to "look over a subordinate's shoulder," to repeat explanations, to make sure she or he is doing the job properly and with dispatch, and occasionally to help personally in the doing. Unless tasks are particularly long and difficult, and especially important, a qualified subordinate adequately trained should be expected to complete an assignment, once explained and understood, without the superior's help in the doing. A finished work product should be turned in whether that be a set of sketches or a sales plan or an inventory count or a routine accounting report. There is something wrong when subordinates continually seek help in carrying out their tasks, or in making decisions that should be theirs to make. There is something wrong if, for example, a manager is always busy looking over initial drafts of a report, improving format and content, and correcting figures, grammar, spelling, and punctuation for her subordinates. That's "upward delegation," guaranteed to keep a manager working long hours and weekends, and keeping her from doing what she should be spending her time on. Only infrequently should a manager pitch in with the doing of work assigned—because of an unusual and very temporary overload of work, pressing deadlines, or exceptional staff shortages. A manager may *sometimes* want to get involved personally, however, when new methods, procedures, or equipment are being tested or installed.

If a manager expects to be promoted she should have someone, preferably more than one person, among her subordinates able to replace her. Thus Ann Hawley, branch manager of a bank, despite an excellent record, was not initially promoted to the management of a larger branch when it became available. She had no replacement prepared to take over her operation. Ann was disappointed, but she learned from the experience. She rectified the situation and eventually she did get transferred to a larger branch, but not as quickly as might have been.

The adequate delegation of responsibility and in most cases jointly with it authority helps both the process of getting out work and morale. Women apparently tend to be less willing than men to delegate responsibilities to subordinates. This has been discussed in Chapter 3. The following builds on that discussion.

Accepting responsibility for what your subordinates do is part of the female manager's job. Putting the blame on a subordinate for something gone wrong does not absolve a manager. It can only lower the esteem in which the manager is held by those above her in the organization. Nor does it help the morale of the subordinate group. After all, it was the group's manager who hired and trained, or approved the hiring and training of, or retained the blamed subordinate. And even if a manager had no choice in hiring or training or retaining an incompetent, or in assigning duties and work to that incompetent, the rules of the game still call for her to shoulder the blame for an incompetent's errors, just as she gets credit along with the subordinates for a very capable subordinate's accomplishments.

Backing up those who work for her in what they do is important to an organization woman's boss' view of her as a manager. It's also important to her subordinates in terms of their backing her up with their loyalty. Top management generally feels that women back up their subordinates about as well as do men, and possibly a little more so.

Managers learn from their mistakes. One of the most difficult lessons an executive must master is that of allowing a subordinate manager to learn by being permitted to make mistakes. That's one of the ingredients in fostering the growth of a subordinate, particularly of one who is being prepared for upward progress in the organization.

It's hard to sit by and do nothing, knowing that Jane, one of your subordinate managers, has made a wrong decision and is going to invest time and company money in something that you know won't work. If it's a lot of time and money you'll veto her decision regardless. If the amounts are more modest, maybe you'd better let her learn from sad experience, if she's going to develop. That's how you learned too!

6

Opportunities—
Making Them, Spotting Them, Seizing Them

Readiness

What does it take for a woman to get ahead in her company? Assuming adequate qualifications and performance, the single most important factor relates to "male chauvinism" on the part of those who run the organization—who are generally males. The attitude of top management toward the progress of women, and the amount of energy top management expends in pushing for women's progress in a company are basic. This has been discussed in Chapter 4. Also noted was the role of "affirmative action." This has definitely been helpful in the bending and shaping of management attitude, and in countering traditional chauvinism.

The freedom and willingness a woman has to pursue her career vigorously is also of basic importance, again assuming adequate qualifications and performance. For maximum progress, this means an ability and willingness to give the career priority as to effort, time, and geographic location. (On the latter, transfers and moves are likely to be an integral part of career progress in the corporate world—for the ambitious). Priority means precedence over personal needs and desires, the needs and desires of a spouse, the spouse's career, and children.

If her ambitions are great, a woman may even find it necessary, as with a man, to adapt her personal life style, her associations, her philosophy, and conceivably her ethics to the requirements of those ambitions—to conformance with the standards of her employer and its top management. She may even end up literally "marrying" her company and divorcing her husband. The interactions of marriage and career are discussed in Chapter 10.

Even for modest ambitions there are a number of specific factors to keep in mind that influence a woman's progress. These have been discussed in Chapters 2 and 3—factors like a professional attitude; and avoiding emotionalism, sensitivity to criticism, and personalization of business decisions. She needs to approach her job with an attitude of cooperation—"fitting in" and getting along with her co-workers—bosses, peers, and subordinates. The organization woman needs to refrain from the use of sex to get special favors. She may also have to accept the existence in her company of some degree of male chauvinism, discrimination and unequal treatment, plus occasional sexual harassment; and determine to deal with their presence—changing employers where the difficulties are intransigent.

The woman—especially if she wants to get ahead as a line manager (command position in operations or sales) in her organization, rather than in a staff position (advisory specialist or "assistant to")—needs a managerial outlook and temperament. She needs to have a desire and ability to supervise, to manage, and to motivate. She must deal with bosses, peers, and subordinates on a "company-viewpoint" basis, rationally, though sometimes also politically, uncolored by personal likes and dislikes, or preconceived opinions and biases.

The managerial woman needs decisiveness, while avoiding inflexibility; a willingness to delegate; and an ability to work under pressure, to live with crises. She should have the kind of temperament which will allow her to take calculated risks and cope with the consequences of adverse results.

To get ahead, the career woman needs a willingness to take on new responsibilities, or new jobs. It helps to be willing to move to new locations when promotions or company decisions require it. The organization woman's attitude must be such that she is willing to work harder and longer hours than men in comparative jobs. Again—if she is strongly ambitious, she must be prepared to give priority to the job and to company wishes, not to her personal preferences, family, or "outside" interests.

Education and technical skills count. Often even more important are "people" skills—the ability to work with people, cooperate, elicit cooperation from others, minimize unfruitful conflict, create confidence, reassure, inspire, motivate, soothe, articulate, persuade, and if need be, compromise.

Where the Opportunities Lie

Opportunity is invaluable to a woman's getting ahead. An opening must exist, open up, or be created, if a promotion is to be obtained. As one woman puts it, it's helpful to "have an appropriate opportunity occur." Or as another says, in reference to creating an opportunity, "there must be a small space available, a need where a woman with confidence and ambition can skip into. Once in she'll have tremendous opportunity." In that respect special skills can help.

Opportunity depends on "being in the right place at the right time"—when an opportunity occurs. That also requires, however, quoting from male executives surveyed: "Appropriate exposure to a diverse part of the organization;" "active participation and exposure to executives during meetings, business trips, etc." Other quotes, from women, along similar lines: "Exposure to upper management;" "visibility with the influential;" "ability to have access to policy makers." Further, it is most helpful "to get a position in decision-making—not just a token position." There is then an opportunity for performance that will provide "visibility to superiors."

Members of the hierarchy promote those they know personally. This is the importance of exposure, within and outside the organization.

When an opportunity does open up, the woman should not hesitate to take the initiative. "Tell your boss you are ready for advancement" [to that opening] (woman vice president). A "reluctance to show ambition" doesn't get promotions (another woman executive).

Situations to be avoided: One where with "slowing growth of the company . . . [there is a] reduction in the number of advancement opportunities;" "small company with no real opportunity for advancement;" "would have to replace two other women who are not about to step down and out;" "too many managers [already overloaded so] not enough opportunities [left];" "corporation with many senior people in the [only] forty to fifty age group [and you're going to have to wait a long time therefore for opportunities to occur at the senior level, the filling of which would then trigger additional opportunities at then-vacated middle levels];" " . . . obstacles also facing men, i.e., relatively young age of existing upper management." "The greatest obstacle for any mid-level executive, male or female, is waiting for a higher level position to open up."

Thoughts to keep in mind (from men, about their irritations with some women): "Impatient about getting ahead;" and "unrealistic expectations for advancement at faster rates than men in similar positions."

Advancement is likely to be the fastest where existing opportunities are many and new ones arise frequently. Advancement is also likely to be faster in a field, area, industry, or company where the competition is limited or relatively weak than where competitors, male or female, in comparison to the number of opportunities, are many, smart, and aggressive.

Where do the opportunities within a given company lie for the woman who wants to advance, to build a career? For a clue it may be worth looking at where the jobs for better-paid women now are to be found, even while recognizing that where they now exist does not necessarily correspond to where they will exist in the future.

To determine where the jobs lie male executives were asked where in their companies the greatest number of the better-paid women are to be found. The most frequent response, that of one-third of the men, was that the greatest number are in "general or office administration." The second most frequent response was that the greatest number of the higher-paid women in their companies are found in marketing and related activities—marketing, market research, sales, promotion, advertising, and public relations. Next came "personnel" and the "accounting and finance" areas. EDP (electronic data processing, that is, computer and computer-related work) was mentioned by a lesser number. Operations (producing products/services sold) was the least mentioned area, except for a scattering of others—mostly engineering, research and development, and legal.

Organization women in the course of their upward climb in the corporate world do not generally stay with one company. Most have changed employers at least once or twice. Only 12 percent are still with their first employer; 88 percent are about evenly divided between those who have had either one or two previous employers, and those who have had at least three employers prior to their present one. Just over two-fifths have been with their present employer more than 10 years, the rest mostly under 5 years.

The first or current job certainly need not be the last. Movement from one employer to another is not only possible, but may well be advantageous if one is not happy with the present one.

What kind of a job have successful organization women started with when they began their careers? The *first* full-time job ever held by the older women was mostly a clerical, bookkeeping, typing, or secretarial position. The younger successful women have most commonly started in a job requiring a college education or else, to a lesser degree, a special talent or skill; mostly in some kind of a supervisory or administrative job, or as a management trainee. A few of both older and younger women started in sales, or as a sales clerk, or in customer service. Very few of both the older and younger began in blue-collar jobs.

With their current employers most organization women, old and young, began in a supervisory or administrative job, or with enrollment as trainee therefor; or in a specialized staff or technical position.

How were these jobs obtained? In one-third of the cases the

starting job with the current employer was obtained by the organization woman through referral by someone she knew—mostly men, and mostly people associated with either her current or a former employer. In over a fifth of the cases a professional recruiter or employment agency was involved. For the rest, the starting job was obtained chiefly through mail or telephone or personal inquiry by the woman, or by answering ads. Some of the more recent female college graduates got their start through school-arranged interviews.

The most likely path by which women reach jobs paying $25,000 and more annually is through internal promotion. Professional recruiters and employment agencies constitute the second most likely path. Their importance goes up, as the salaries paid increase, though even for really high salaries internal promotion outranks them. Referrals from company employees, associates, and others, are the third most popular route of advancement. This is followed by applicant ads and applicant telephone/mail/personal inquiries.

Bosses and Mentors

The organization women surveyed were asked to check off how they got promoted to their present jobs, other than by ability and performance. The replies clearly indicate that the boss plays a major role. Almost half of the women were recommended for their promotions by the boss, and almost half of those to *his* job. Either he had himself gotten a promotion to a new position, or had retired or resigned. Mentors also appear to play a significant role in women's promotions. So does affirmative action. A fair number of the women created the jobs to which they were elevated. They either expanded old jobs into new and more important ones, or they found a need and thus a new position in the organization which they could fill.

For 95 percent of the organization women surveyed, the boss is a man, and he can do a lot to get a woman promoted when an opening occurs. As I have noted, almost half of the women queried got themselves promoted to their present jobs through recommendation by the boss. And of the 81 percent of the women who claim that at least one individual had been outstandingly helpful to them in their careers, in most cases this individual was their boss. In some additional cases he was the boss' boss, who presumably knew of her through her immediate boss.

If the boss is going places, the woman working for him has a chance to do the same. If not, she may very well be stuck where she is. "Working for a boss who's not progressing," as one woman manager puts it, is a big handicap. Occasionally too, one may be working for a boss who *is* progressing, but is not a very nice guy. If a woman does too good a job for him, he may deliberately hold her back from promotion to something better or from transfer to something potentially better. She is too useful to him in her present job. Either way, with the boss who's not progressing, or with the not-so-nice guy who is, the woman is in a tough spot. She should find another boss, whether with her present employer or another one.

Mentors can be instrumental in a career, whether it be the boss who doubles as a mentor, or the boss' boss, or someone else. The mentor acts as a confidant, a coach, an influential supporter and a friend, in the organization woman's struggle to succeed in her career. As one senior male executive enunciated his view of the mentor's role for the woman: "I cannot adequately emphasize the importance of mentors; [a real obstacle to a woman's getting ahead is the] absence of mentors who truly understand the predominantly male work world as seen by both men and women." Another expresses a similar thought: "Finding senior executives to serve in mentor role [is critical to the progress of women in my firm]." The following are three of the comments by women voicing the need for "A strong mentor; solid relationship with several key members of senior management;" "at least one mentor—especially a male, influential one;" and "strong support from a top male executive."

Insofar as a mentoring relationship represents a commitment by the mentor to the woman as his protégé, the mantle of his prestige and power in the organization helps to promote her acceptance, to diminish her rejection, by the men in the company. The mentor's role as teacher helps. So does his ability to facilitate the opening of doors and the discovery and seizure of opportunities. He can make progress in the hierarchy much easier for the woman. (That's also true for a male protégé.)

Zey in his book *The Mentor Connection* points out that "Mentoring has a Catch-22 quality about it. To be chosen as a protégé, a person must already appear to be a 'rising star' who can enhance the mentor's career."[17] A mentor is more likely to be interested in a prospective protégé if he feels that the woman he sponsors has something to offer in terms of special skills, intelligence, and abilities. He is encouraged to take on a protégé if he feels these attributes can be developed and utilized, and that their utilization will directly or indirectly reflect favorably upon and help his own position and objectives in the organization.

Zey refers to the presence in male/female mentoring of the problems of innuendo and sexual involvement; and the suspicious spouse. Sometimes getting a spouse together with the "other woman" or the "other man" so they get to know each other, and being open and communicative about the mentoring situation can be helpful. Spousal relationships do appear generally to survive the corporate ones, though not without publicized exceptions. On another aspect, Zey quotes one male corporate executive: "Acquire more than one female protégé, and you will then be perceived as a people developer, not a womanizer."[18]

It is well to have more than one mentor in an organization. What happens if there is only one mentor and he is transferred to another part of a large organization—one where from his new position the mentor can't do much for the protégé? What happens if a mentor falls out of favor, and he is the only mentor; or if there is none other who in the circumstances can or will offer protection? The tie to the fallen *can* hurt the protégé. That's the negative side of mentoring.

Further Strategies

Networking too is important. The term refers to a web of friendly contacts with people who may be useful in providing technical and other information or advice on the job; or in providing leads, other information, and recommendations on job or promotion opportunities inside and outside one's present organization. That web of contacts had better heavily include men, not merely other women. Note that 86 percent of the organization women surveyed claim the one individual who's been outstandingly helpful to them in their career was a man. Only 14 percent claim that individual was a woman. Even a greater percentage, 96 percent, claim the individual who gave them the promotion to their present job was a man. The corporate world *is* still a man's world.

Two quotes from management women emphasize the importance of "establishing a good peer network and good upward visibility;" and "including key men in your network of contacts so you will know where the job opportunities are."

If the career woman is to create opportunities for herself she must be able to compete with men in respect to education, skills, and experience required for a job. Inadequacy in these is the second most frequently mentioned obstacle, by both the men and women surveyed, to a woman's getting ahead in an organization. It ranks next to male chauvinism (discussed in Chapter 4). In some cases "affirmative action" may temporarily give a woman an advantage despite inadequacies in those respects. Even so, the inadequacies are going to have to be overcome, perhaps in part through experience gained in jobs which a woman would not have had the opportunity to hold without the initial push of affirmative action.

In some respects experience and the skills that come with it present a "Catch-22" situation—the woman cannot get a higher job without experience plus skills developed in a lower-level job, yet tradition and discrimination have kept her from getting the preceding lower-rung job needed to qualify her for the higher job.

The importance of continuous upgrading of education and skills, formal and informal, for the next job as well as the present one, needs to be stressed for everyone, but particularly for women. If one is going to create opportunities for herself she needs to prepare herself for them. As noted in Chapter 2, time needs to be set aside for courses, seminars, trade, and professional meetings, "reading up" and as part of networking, cultivating those who can be helpful with information and advice on matters bearing on one's job and career, present and future.

Comments by a few of the men surveyed in respect to upgrading women's qualifications to fill the better jobs are: "Many are improperly prepared to handle assigned responsibilities, both from education and experience perspective." "Those [women] who constantly complain about not being promoted, but do nothing to prepare for it." "No technical understanding." "Finding enough of them [women for better jobs] with needed qualifications." "Getting them [women] to broaden their backgrounds and career goals—they tend to want to stay in 'comfortable' assignments."

7

Cutting Your Losses

Reasons to Change Jobs

Insofar as economic or other circumstances permit, a woman should consider seriously now, not 10 years hence, whether she ought to change employers. The difference between a brilliant career and a dead-end job can lie in "picking" the right or wrong company and the right or wrong boss.

A woman does have to determine first, of course, what her priorities are. What is it realistically that is most important to her and to what degree—a career, what kind of career, doing what; money, and what kind of money; "power", prestige, or other satisfactions; marriage, children; present friends, social ties, activities, and the leisure to enjoy them; and preferred geographic location.

What does she *want* to achieve in a career? What is it that she can *hope* to achieve, and what can she realistically *expect* to achieve—given her present or attainable training, skills, experience, intelligence, personal characteristics, marital status, age, and circumstances. She should consider the direct and indirect price she may have to pay for what she wants, then plan and proceed accordingly.

In your own case, begin by considering where you are now situated, the boss you have, and possible transfers within the company. Then look at the industry of which the company, or the segment of the company for which you work, is part. Is it growing, stable, or declining? What is the competition likely to be in the future, domestic and foreign? What is technology and innovation likely to do? Changes in public taste and buying habits? Changes in government policy as to procurement from the industry, or in regulations affecting the industry? In general, what kind of a future does the industry have?

Similarly, if you're a specialist rather than a generalist, what is the future for your field of expertise—whether procurement, merchandising, market research, editing, computer programming, design, advertising, public relations, economic analysis, accounting, engineering, law, or biochemistry? What can it lead to, in your industry or in other industries?

As to your present employer, what is the future of your company, and of the segment of the company in which you are employed? What about the company's financial strength, its management, its future competitive position and profitability? Is it likely to increase, maintain, or lose its share of the industry's market? Is it likely to grow through diversification or acquisitions, or is it likely itself to be acquired by another concern?

What about your *liking* for your job, as well as for the company? What are the avenues and potential for promotion—considering your position as line or staff, the department and functions in the company in which promotion opportunities are greatest; the number of opportunities; the age of superiors to whose positions you may aspire; policy on promotions from within versus outside the organization; and the roles of seniority, education and degrees, merit, and politics? What about attitudes of company management towards employees generally, and toward women in particular?

What about the boss? Do you like him? Is he respected? Is he going places? If so, you have a much better chance yourself. What is his attitude towards subordinates, and towards you in particular? Is he noted for getting his subordinates promoted? Or is he the occasional selfish superior who is going to avoid getting you promoted, if you're too useful to him where you are?

Signs of a job's potential or lack of any can be detected. Sometimes just the circumstances of entry have a bearing. Entry into a management training program promises a greater future with an employer than entry as a file clerk or a typist. Entry into a sales job, where most top management people have come out of the company's sales department and continue to be recruited from sales, is obviously more likely to lead to success than entry into a production job if few executives started in that function. A job supervising clerical employees performing routine chores is less likely to lead upward than a lower-paying job as a salesperson in the same firm.

An impressive title is not a substitute for substance in the job one holds. It is meaningful responsibility and authority which is important. So is exposure to people in higher management, and an opportunity for a woman to exhibit her abilities to those who can promote or cause others to promote. That opportunity is a sign of potential in a job. Its absence may point to a job that is dead-end.

The presence of too many young people in too many high-level jobs, unless in a fast-growth situation, serves to block avenues of promotion and one may be better off elsewhere.

Job history may indicate a career has dead-ended. How long have you been in your present job, and how long has it been since your last promotion? How long have others before you, in your present job, taken to achieve promotions and how high have they gone? Forecasting from history into the future, unless conditions in the company have changed radically, is about as good a way as any for determining how long it is going to take you to climb, and just how far the climb is likely to go. Similarly, looking at what has happened to others in other industries and companies is one way of judging what opportunities there may be elsewhere—adjusting for likely changes in industry and company growth rates.

Timing

Most employees, men as well as women, after working for the same employer for some years, are in danger of being "locked in" permanently with their employment situation. It becomes difficult after a long period of time to switch from one industry to another.

So also it is difficult after years in a staff position to get transferred to a line position in the same company, or to find a line position with another company. (The reverse, going from line to staff, is less hard, but still not easy either.) It's tough after a long time in accounting to change to sales, or to transform oneself from an advertising specialist to a procurement agent. One gets chained to an industry, a specialty, or to a company. It therefore is urgent for one who does want to change to act while there is still time to make the desired transition.

A few changes in jobs and companies, even industries, along the way, particularly in one's early career, is not without advantages. It provides desirable experience and perspective. It is likely to be thought an asset by a prospective employer, or the existing employer, when considering an individual for a desired spot. (Too many changes, on the other hand, often classifies an individual as a "job-hopper;" this is a liability with most employers).

The woman who has worked her way up to the "Number One" position in her department or specialty in a company has a problem in seeking further advancement. The head of a company's advertising department finds further progress in her company is blocked. The marketing vice president of a firm is similarly blocked, as is the head of a firm's public relations group, and an apparel manufacturer's chief designer. Number One finds it necessary in most cases to accept her existing position as terminal. This may be quite satisfying. If not, however, she may try to expand the activities of her group, thus the number of her subordinates, and thus her pay and the importance of her position. Or, if she is not yet completely locked in, if she is in a staff position she may try to get transferred to a line management position—either at headquarters or out in the field with a branch or district—or if she's in a line job, from line in one division of a multidivision company to line in a more important or larger division if she is still young enough to make that transition. Alternatively, Number One may find it becomes necessary to search for a position similar to her present one, but with a larger firm, one that has a larger advertising or marketing or public relations or design group than the present employer.

Assume that a woman manager or professional decides that her career has come to a halt where she is. She decides to change employers while there is still time. She will not be alone. As indicated in the previous chapter, only 12 percent of the organization women surveyed are still with their first employer. Fully 88 percent are not. These are evenly divided between those who have had either one or two previous employers, and those who have had at least three employers prior to their present one. The first or current job need not be the last.

If one is considering a job with another company one should try to check out the history and prospects for growth of the prospective new employer. One should also try to check out promotion policy and the history of others like oneself in the new company. A briefing, if it can be gotten, on intra-company political and other factors relevant to future progress in that organization would be useful. This may be difficult to obtain. In respect to such factors there are always unknown risks in going to a new employer. But life is full of risks!

8

Understanding Your Boss

First Priorities

If you're going to get ahead in an organization, it is desirable to understand what motivates your boss and what *his* objectives are. Insofar as your work and ideas promote those objectives you will be advancing your standing with him. He will then be inclined to want to be helpful in advancing your own objectives. Insofar as your work and ideas don't promote his interests he is less likely to be concerned about promoting yours. Understanding your boss's personal goals therefore is of relevance to yours.

The key to understanding your boss is to realize that his first concern is himself, then the company. This holds for your boss, his boss, and his boss's boss, on up to the head of the firm—and back on down to yourself. Your boss's foremost objective is retention of what he already has—his position, compensation, "perks," and authority. His next most important goal is to add to what he has and to his personal happiness. This may include a promotion and more money for himself; a larger office with more luxurious furnishings; more authority; getting rid of a rival; or bringing a pet project to a successful conclusion. Gains for the organization (the group or department or company he heads) constitute the boss's lesser priority, ranking after his own security of position and personal fulfillment. What's good for the boss comes before what's good for the company. Of course gains for the organization may be among the things that are good for the boss. But where there is a conflict of interest "personal" comes first.

Eastman, Mills and Winokur[19] summed it up in *Equal To The Task* in their Law of Self-Preservation. "It is ingenuous to make assumptions that your co-workers are principally concerned with common or company goals. Everyone [including your boss] is concerned first with his/her own gain or loss in any situation."

Some years ago Mary Gamlin was put in charge of the southeastern branch of a national drug wholesaler. She replaced a man who had been with the company for many years and had managed the branch for the past 5 years. He had turned in what was considered to be a reasonably good performance. Profits had increased on an average of about 8 to 9 percent annually. At age sixty-five he had now retired.

Mary had been his assistant. Put in charge of the branch she now felt free to try out some ideas she had long held, but had been unable to get her former boss to try. She was also willing to work a lot harder than her former boss. That boss, as he approached retirement, had been inclined to coast along. Market growth and minimal operating improvements, with only a modest effort, had combined to produce a respectable profit increase year to year.

After a few months it became evident to Mary that with considerable changes, which she as yet had only partially made in the internal operations of the branch, she could cut costs considerably. Together with some additional sales effort she could this year more than double the profits of the previous year. This posed a problem, however. A fairly good improvement was tolerable. A doubling of performance could be dangerous. It would lead her company to expect similar or at least very substantial annual profit increases in the future. She doubted that after an initial spectacular jump profit increases could be expected to continue at more than possibly 10 to 15 percent a year, and even that rate would be difficult to maintain. Moreover, tough new competition might be coming in the next year.

What did Mary Gamlin decide to do? She could cut profits this year down to a more modest, but laudable, increase of 12 percent above the prior year. Thus she could hold up on some planned cost reductions. She could continue with increased sales efforts, but keep them down to a modest level. She could spend more money on sales training programs and on sales meetings, more than was really profitable. She could provide one-time special bonuses to key people. She could add money to the advertising budget this year, more than was needed or likely fruitful. And she could continue to keep some "dead wood" on the payroll. Cutting this year's profit increase to 12 percent would enable her almost certainly to produce similar further profit increases in the following year, and the next. She did exactly that. Her company was happy and she was happy.

Mary did not try immediately, nor next year, nor the next, to produce peak profits for the company. She was more concerned about the effects of her efforts on her own situation. What was best for her was more important than what was best for the company. In a sense she had learned a lesson from her former boss. He had known what *could* be done—she had told him and urged him to try some of her ideas, but had never convinced him to adopt them. She now understood why. Expediency and a manager's self-interest take precedence over the employer's interests.

Mary Gamlin's old boss had increased profits of his branch at the rate of 8 to 9 percent annually. Mary had upped this to 12 percent. Both had discerned that which managers do occasionally sense—if they do an outstanding job this year they make it tougher for themselves the following year. The boss does not look for a subordinate to perform spectacularly in any one year. He does want "reasonably" good results, however, and that in turn is what his boss wants, and on up to what the board of directors and the stockholders want of the head of the firm.

"Reasonably" good is commonly that percentage increase in profits (or increase in sales or output per employee, or decrease in cost) which has held, on average, in the last several years, with heaviest emphasis on the most recent history. Business conditions, inflation, other major factors, and how others—competitors, other managers—perform, of course affects the definition of what is "reasonably" good. Steady reasonable progress is the key to survival, bonuses, and advancement in the business organization. The organization woman should understand that as with Gamlin, modest but consistent annual improvements in achievement may be preferable to the greater average, but more erratic increases she is likely to obtain year to year if she strives always for peak results. Constant stable progress is easier on the nerves than drastic ups and downs. It's a lot more pleasant, and could be more productive for her personally.

Turning in a spectacular performance in any one year, or merely in general doing a really outstanding job has another aspect to it. The woman manager ought to be aware of it, though it should not necessarily prevent her from putting out her best efforts on the job. The eager innocent who shows up by her own excellent performance the mediocrity of her peers, whether in the executive suite or on the supervisory level or on the assembly line, is not always applauded. Her colleagues will do their best to disable her. They won't always succeed, but they will sometimes.

Because your boss's first interest is himself, *any idea or action you may recommend or initiate will be considered by him in terms of its costs, benefits, and risks to himself personally.* Costs, benefits, and risks to the company or to the function which he heads count; but *first* for their effect on himself, and only *secondarily* for their effect on the stockholders. This may lead to turning down some of your ideas if they are good for the company, but not in your boss's opinion good for your boss. This is especially true where innovative and entrepreneurial thinking or other risk-taking ideas are involved.

Assessing the Risk Factor

As already referred to, the first concern of bosses generally, and this is likely to include your boss, is the safe retention of what he has. This means taking risks to make more money for his company is less important than the safety of his personal status quo. His actions are ruled by the desire to avoid potential problems, and not to gamble with new ideas or investment trying to achieve the best possible performance.

The antipathy to risk means there will be a tendency to discourage innovation and entrepreneurship. It means a boss is likely to have a bias against ideas and actions which don't conform to the customary wisdom and thinking in the firm. Innovation is instituting something new; or making changes in an existing product, process, or procedure. Entrepreneurship differs, though it may be based on innovation. It is the ability to see an opportunity and to grasp and successfully exploit it. Both innovation and entrepreneurial action involve risks.

An innovation may turn out to be unworkable. If it *is* feasible, it must be sold; the market must accept it. An innovation may adversely affect a firm's present investments. And it can mean danger to an organization's hierarchy. An innovation can hurt those who fought it. It can threaten those who were in a position to think of it first and should have, but didn't. A new product can diminish the importance of executives who have been associated with the production and sale of older products, which now may be displaced by the new, especially if the new is to be handled by a different set of executives. The internal political ramifications can be considerable. If you have an innovative or entrepreneurial-type idea, something new, keep in mind therefore the many risk potentials which exist, not least the last—the political.

The hazards for your boss in new ideas are particularly great if you ask him to consider something that is contrary to the conventional thinking of his superiors or of his peers. You're asking a lot. Suppose he follows one of your suggestions. Suppose further it turns out to be good. The prospective rewards your boss can expect may not be adequate in his thinking to balance out the loss of face plus the direct or indirect penalties he may incur if the suggestion turns out to be bad. Even if your suggestion proves highly profitable, there may be a drawback—the resentment of those whose conventional thinking has been shown up to be wrong.

The boss *will* listen to your ideas and *will* take risks if he believes the potential rewards for success are great, penalties for failure are low, and the risks are small. He will also gamble when he feels risk-taking is his least hazardous course. This is the case when he comes to believe that without drastic action involving risk he may not personally survive a poor performance against more innovative risk-taking competitors.

Bosses do tend to avoid risk. Nevertheless bosses *need* occasional risk-carrying innovative ideas. The payoff for innovation can be considerable, and there are times when the penalties for its lack can also be considerable. So, if you as a managerial or professional woman do have such ideas, the boss *can* be sold on them.

How? First, if it can be done quietly and without upsetting your superior, and if it is appropriate, test your ideas with peers, mentors, network contacts, or others whose judgment you respect. If after that you believe your ideas are sound and feasible, put together a presentation to be made to your boss, oral or written, informal or formal, simple or elaborate, as you think most suitable.

Discuss the ideas with the boss. Give him your analysis of the benefits, costs, and risks. Try to tie in your ideas with what you know of the ideas or philosophy he himself has previously expressed. He's more apt to approve if he considers your ideas to be somehow extensions of, similar to, or at least consistent with his own. (As to credit for the ideas, if he says "yes" and then tries to pass off your ideas as his, knowledge of your authorship is still likely to leak sooner or later. In any case the boss, who can considerably influence your future, will know where the ideas originated).

If a company's competitor, or someone higher up in your organization, or persons the boss respects or believes in are already doing something like what you propose, refer to that. A senior executive of a major cosmetics firm in private conversation some years ago confessed that the best way she had found to convince her president to increase expenditures on a market research program was to point out what the other major competitors were spending—with the response by the president: "Are you sure what you are proposing is adequate?"

Figure out how your ideas may contribute to the boss's satisfactions—his desires for promotion, money, authority and influence, reputation and recognition (status), love of challenge, feeling of accomplishment. Appeal to those.

If the boss appears less than enthusiastic try to avoid pressing and getting an immediate "no." Let him think about it. Even with a definite "no," go back to the drawing board. Try to put together more information and data which in the light of the boss's objections may be helpful in changing his mind. Try also to figure out how to minimize the risks, as by experimenting on a small scale. Approach your boss again later, or sooner if it's opportune. A "no" *can* sometimes be turned into a "yes."

Julie Randall was promotion manager for a large cookie bakery. Some years ago in a meeting with her boss she suggested the bakery produce and sell a line of cookies specially baked and packaged for Christmas. Her superior disagreed. He believed sales volume would be limited, the costs would be relatively high, and the expense of taking back and giving credit for cookies unsold after the holiday would be high (company policy was to take back and credit unsold product).

Julie was not discouraged. She believed in her idea. She persisted in bringing it up, along with additional figures each time to show the idea could be profitable. She also suggested that two things be done to minimize the risk of loss. Only that amount of cookies would be baked in a first trial as could be pre-sold to major supermarket customers at a larger-than-normal markup over cost, and with an understanding that no returns of unsold product would be accepted. Further, the first trial would take place the Christmas following the one in the current year. A "disaster" test would be conducted in the current year's holiday season. A small amount of cookies would be placed in a limited number of test stores to see what happened. If sales results were not good the idea would be dropped and a possible marketing failure the next Christmas thereby avoided.

On the basis of minimized risk her boss finally reluctantly approved. The idea was presented to the firm's New Products Committee and it went along with it. Now after 4 years the sales of Christmas cookies far exceed what Julie had hoped for, and the line contributes substantially to the bakery's profits.

If ideas are turned down and you feel strongly enough about them it sometimes pays to "plant seeds" (the ideas) with mentors, the boss's peers, and others. You do have to be careful, of course, since in a way you're going over the boss's head.

Alice Williams was head of a company's community relations program. She suggested to her boss that as part of the company's program a given number of dollars be devoted to encourage local artists. The boss thought the dollars would be better spent in other directions. Alice did not take "no" for an answer. While contacting community leaders on various matters she discussed her ideas on local artists, getting reactions and planting seeds. The seeds matured and some months later with the help of community backing she was able to demonstrate that dollars set aside to encourage local artists would engender a considerable amount of good will for the company. The boss was convinced and the dollars were forthcoming.

An apparel chain's store manager, Betty Dillon, believed she could considerably increase her store's sales of sportswear by changing the standardized space allocations and displays within the area assigned to that merchandise. To do so she required approval from her boss and the staff at chain headquarters. Getting approval was a complicated affair and somewhat uncertain. Betty believed her ideas were good and decided to go ahead on her own—without informing headquarters and getting approval first. She ran her own "experiment," changing things around. (Only headquarters staff "experts" were supposed to run experiments). Sportswear sales increased by one-third. Headquarters learned of it and was miffed by the lack of prior consent, but forgave her. The store manager's new ideas were applied to other stores. A little later the innovator was rewarded with the management of a larger store at a substantially higher salary.

As with Betty Dillon, there are times when a manager may want to try out an idea without first letting the boss know about it and getting his authorization. She may believe the boss won't approve, yet feels strongly that the idea is good and is needed. It may be a matter of changing the format of a company newspaper or of the sales brochures sent to company branches. It may be an innovation which violates a long-standing tradition. It may be an investment requiring a fair amount of money. The manager is taking a calculated risk in not first informing the boss and getting his approval. Yet if the new format or the innovation or the investment is successful the manager is likely to be forgiven the lack of prior consent, and may be well rewarded. If it's not successful . . . well, that's the risk. Sometimes it takes risks to reap rewards.

9

Understanding the Organization

When Things Are not what They Seem

The organization woman should understand her organization as well as her boss. For instance, power is supposed to flow from the top down in clearly defined fashion from one echelon to another. Duties and responsibilities are carefully delineated. The organization chart accurately reflects the structure of a firm.

All of this may or may not be true. Ambiguity in an enterprise is not at all uncommon. Positions on an organization chart and titles, for example, can be misleading. At one time the president of a large oil company took his orders from one of his vice presidents. That vice president represented the largest single ownership of stock in the company. And the No. 2 man in a billion-dollar industrial organization, the largest in its industry, is not even listed on the company payroll. He is the personal attorney of the dominating chairman of the board.

Executives with minimal influence in a corporation may include people with impressive titles and impressive-sounding duties, individuals who have been "kicked upstairs." They possess imposing embellishments which hide the brutal fact that a shift in financial control of the company, market changes, poor performance, pure company politics, or some combination of these has stripped them of the very considerable authority they once did have. Yet because retention of their abilities and expertise, their following among employees and customers, and their loyalty to the company is of some importance to their successors in power, they have not been fired. Face-saving via title and office space is deemed worthwhile.

Occasional ambiguity at the top is matched in lower echelons too. For a woman who wants to get ahead, a little checking around to learn just where power and influence lie in the organization, and particularly in that part of the organization which most directly affects her, is of some importance. It's a first step in learning to be aware of the political aspects that will affect her climb up the corporate ladder.

A line manager is one who has the authority and responsibility for the making or selling of a product or the performance and sale of a service which a company provides to its customers. A staff manager, on the other hand, provides specialized skills, knowledge and advice, and checks (auditing, quality control) to help the line manager. A director of manufacturing and a sales manager are line. A quality manager, a manager of procurement and a personnel director are staff.

Most organization women hold staff positions. Less than one-fourth of the women surveyed hold line jobs. Almost half have not more than three persons reporting directly or indirectly to them, and three-fifths have not more than five. Of survey respondents 30 percent do claim to have over 10 people reporting to them directly or through subordinates. Twenty percent, one-fifth of those surveyed, claim authority over more than 20 persons. (Most of those over whom authority is held are women. However, for 12 percent of the organization women, 70 percent or more of those under them are men).

The better-paying jobs in an organization generally are in line management, not staff. For the organization woman who is starting out, therefore, it may be worth considering a lower starting salary in a line job, rather than a higher salary in staff, if the line in her company holds promise of a greater future. It should be noted that after a few years in a staff job one gets to be stamped as staff. Transfer from a staff to a line position then becomes difficult.

Within an organization an individual woman manager may be given a greater or lesser amount of independence in the way she operates her department. The degree to which she is allowed to operate freely, making her own decisions, will not necessarily be the same as that permitted other managers at similar levels in the hierarchy. How much she is supervised is determined by how her boss judges the effectiveness of the department which she heads, and by her boss's degree of confidence in her. Another factor is the busyness of the boss. If the boss's attention is divided among many subordinates, or is concentrated on problems outside her area, she is more likely to be left alone than when the boss has lots of free time for "supervising."

MBO and the Career Woman

In running an organization top management has extensively employed what is known as MBO, management by objectives. MBO has often been misused. It's not always a blessing. The organization woman should be careful and a little skeptical in dealing with it.

Management by objectives makes use of spelled-out written objectives, commonly for one year ahead, which managers are supposed to try to achieve. It starts with objectives at the corporate level and works down to objectives for the various divisions, departments, and other units of the organization. It is based on the hope that they will motivate managers to be more effective than would be the case without them. It should be noted, however, that for a *good* manager formal objectives may not matter. For a *bad* manager formal objectives also may not matter, very much. Will the existence of official objectives really change the ability of a manager to manage?

Objectives can be set too high. Sales quotas which are

realistically unreachable by most of those on a sales force may result in less, not greater sales efforts. Quota participants, aware that the goals are fanciful, won't even begin to try to reach for what they *know* is unattainable. Objectives also can be set too low, calling for only minimum efforts to meet them. Maximum exertion is not encouraged by goals too easily met.

Goals need to be set high enough to require some effort to achieve them, yet low enough to be realistically attainable by most of those involved. Those involved need also to believe that the goals are reachable. And there should be enough motivation, rewards or satisfactions, to call forth the effort needed to reach the set goals.

What is true of objectives for her organization is also true for the organization woman herself. Her career objectives should be neither too low nor unrealistically high. They should be high enough to require some effort to reach them, yet not so high as to be unattainable and merely a continuous source of defeat and unhappiness. Also, she needs to believe the rewards in money or other satisfactions justify the personal costs required (what else she gives up) to achieve the career objectives she has set for herself.

MBO is often used to evaluate managers by measuring results attained against objectives. This is valid only if results can be truly measured, and if the objectives are really a fair standard against which to measure. Are the objectives set for one manager equally, less, or more difficult to attain than the objectives set for another manager? Only if their objectives are equally difficult of accomplishment can two managers be fairly compared on the basis of achievement of objectives. And how does one really measure difficulty of attainment, let alone compare degrees of attainment for different objectives for different managers in different environments, and with differing degrees of unanticipated good or bad luck (those "intervening variables")? What has an air of objectivity about it, evaluation of a manager's effectiveness on the basis of achievement of written goals, is not at all objective. It is highly subjective, despite a widespread impression to the contrary and its ubiquitous adoption as a wonderful management tool.

A word of warning to the woman manager. If the boss involves you in developing a set of objectives, take it seriously. Don't be too anxious to impress the boss, however, by eagerly agreeing to overambitious objectives. Your performance may later be appraised by comparison with those same objectives. And additionally, your ability to make realistic projections is likely to be questioned.

Budgets and Forecasts

As part of understanding an organization the woman manager needs to understand the operating budget. This is a schedule of estimated receipts and expenses. For an organization overall and for each segment thereof (division, department, branch, or other unit) the budget matches dollar receipts, from sales or from company allocations of funds, with expenditures.

The budget is a *one-year* plan. As such it encourages *short-run* thinking. It prods a woman manager, when necessary to meet a budget total, to cut expenditures which won't much affect her performance in the current year, though the cuts hurt achievement in later years. Future damage is overbalanced by the need to show desired "numbers," to meet budget totals, this year. This is especially true when her bonus is awarded in considerable measure by current budgetary results. Thus specific expenditure cuts to meet a desired budget total might be made, where applicable, in customer services, in maintenance of buildings and of equipment, in advertising, in research, or in recruiting and training programs. The cuts may be expensive in the long-run, but in the short-run they help a manager to stay within her total budget.

The woman manager should understand that a budget is the product of history. Budgeted totals allocated to each segment of the organization for a current year are heavily influenced by the amounts each has spent in prior years. Funds also tend to be allocated to the different segments according to their *current* rather than their *potential* importance. This plus the history of past allocations is partly why money and efforts are often concentrated more strongly, and for longer than they should be, on older established, but declining products and services; and less strongly on newer, but potentially more important products and services.

The established markets may currently still be producing most of a company's profits. That carries weight, even if the percentage of the profits is declining.

The desires of top management are definitely influential in budget allocations. A company head will tend to fund generously those activities which directly or indirectly further those projects and ideas in which he is personally interested. The woman manager should keep this in mind. What the *competition* spends on particular activities also influences her budget. Thus the organization woman would do well to try to maintain current information on what others in her industry are spending on the activity she manages.

Budgets are influenced by the general economic climate. If the economy is booming and the outlook for business is good, optimism reigns. Then budgets for advertising or training programs or added personnel tend to be generous. The reverse also holds.

Because budgets are determined in part by what a department spent in the past, the woman who has always included some excessive expense in her operation will be rewarded with a larger allocation of money than she really needs. (It's always been in her budget in the past). With minimal effort she can make herself look good, meeting or even underspending her over-generous budget allowance, by cutting a little on the excessive amounts—only she knows they're excessive. A manager who has always operated close to the bone, trying continually to improve performance, has no excess "fat" in reserve. If she runs into unanticipated cost over-runs, she can be in real trouble with her budget.

A manager who comes up with some new ideas for cutting her costs, and does so, may be applauded—this year—but could well be expected to produce like reductions the next year. How does she produce an encore? Will the ambitious but cautious manager perhaps spread her cost-cutting ideas over several years so reductions are not all made in one year? See the Mary Gamlin example in Chapter 8.

Organizations plan one year ahead via the budget. They also plan further ahead, commonly 3 to 10 years, occasionally longer. Such planning starts with an assessment of what the future holds for the products and/or services a company or a division, department, branch, or other unit produces and sells. An assessment is also made of what a company possesses or can obtain in the way of capital, management talent, technology, facilities, manpower, and marketing strength; of where its strengths and weaknesses lie; and of what its alternatives and opportunities are and can be. Planning presupposes that an organization, if it knows what the future holds, can take action now to change what otherwise will happen—to avoid or ease difficulties, and to better take advantage of opportunities.

The organization woman knows that assessing the future is tough. Perhaps one of the easiest approaches, neither the best nor the worst, is the assumption that past trends will continue into the future. This is supplemented by analyses of expected changes in trends, and of new developments.

Perhaps as much as by either history or analyses, forecasts are influenced by the opinions of others—associates, economists, bankers, customers, competitors, politicians, journalists, and even spouses. Of special importance are the opinions and pet ideas of those who run their companies. Technicians, professionals, and women managers (and even "objective" outside consultants and research firms) whose ideas and reports affect company planning are commonly well aware of the desires of the executives they work for. A need to "survive" in the organization and the enhancement of their promotion prospects (continued retention of clients for the outside consultants and researchers) are important to those concerned. They know what those at the top would like to hear, what those in charge don't care to hear, and what projects the top executives would like to include in the planning being done. It's easier to tell the boss (or a client) what he wants to hear than what he doesn't—and the knowledge of what he wants to hear *can* affect estimates of the future and the planning for it that inevitably contain large elements of guesswork.

The best planning is not necessarily that which is most reasonable. The woman manager responsible for coming up with suggested plans for top executive approval needs to consider not only what is best, but also what is acceptable. The desires of important decision makers, the preferences of the board of directors, the prejudices of a company's bankers where there will be a need to borrow heavily, the requirements of the tax laws, and the likely reactions of governmental regulatory agencies, all have to be considered. The internal, not just external, political aspects of alternative plans for the future are part of what is feasible and best. All of this is important for planning, whether on the corporate, divisional, or departmental level. The woman manager should recognize that. Companies, or departments, don't grow or don't decline, live or die, by reason alone. Human factors and emotions—pride, prejudice, desire, faith, fear—play a vital part, for an organization is a living organism.

10

Career and Marriage

Behind the Demographics

In this chapter the interplay between career and marriage will be explored. The majority of the managerial and professional women surveyed are married, as are the majority of all the working women in the nation.

Of the women surveyed, 55 percent are married, 21 percent are separated or divorced, and 20 percent are single. The others are widowed, or are living with a man in an unmarried state. The 55 percent figure for married is a bit lower than the 59 percent figure for all women in the U.S. civilian labor force. The 21 percent figure for separated and divorced is considerably higher than the estimated 15 percent separated and divorced which now holds for all working women.

The high rate of separated and divorced for the relatively successful career women queried does not prove, but could imply, that *combining high career ambition with marriage leads to a high rate of separation and divorce.* That's a possibility, even a probability. There's also the likelihood of another influence. It may be that it is the characteristics and drive which enable women to build successful careers that also tend to lead to their separation and divorce.

Half of the married women among the respondents have children under eighteen. This is similar to the proportion which holds for all married working women in the U.S. Fewer of the separated/divorced among those surveyed, however, have children than the general run of separated and divorced working women in the nation. Perhaps a high priority placed upon success in the career, during marriage, by those in the better-paid positions, substituted in part for the desire to have children, or sidetracked it, and contributed to marriage dissolution.

It is fair to assume that a successful career by no means excludes a successful marriage and children. Nevertheless, it also is fair to assume that *heavy emphasis* placed on a career may cut down on the bearing of children and the continuation of a marriage.

Why Wives Work

Many of the women combining marriage and career surveyed get a great deal of satisfaction from their careers. Yet even of these, women who have good and presumably challenging jobs, fully three-fourths admit that financial considerations are important too. The observation of one highly-paid manager among the women polled exemplifies the point: "My career originated from financial need. I feel that if men met all their family's financial needs, less women would be in the job market. Self-actualization does not necessarily arise out of having a 'job.' "

Nearly one-fourth of the married women among survey respondents believe they would or might quit their careers if money were of no concern. The drop-out potential is similar for those who are separated or divorced. It is a little less for the singles. The now-or-formerly married with children are more likely to quit than those without children.

Regardless, the great majority of even organization career women with children claim they would continue their careers in the absence of financial need. One reason for this may lie in the perceived effect of the career, for most, on the quality of the woman's life. A large majority, 84 percent of those women questioned on this—the now-and-formerly-married—expressed the opinion that a career helped rather than hurt the quality of their lives. The perception of benefit holds, by a wide margin, for the married, the separated and divorced, those with and without children, all ages and all incomes among the respondents. Challenge, pride in the job, getting away from the routine of the house and children, all may be factors. Money undoubtedly is a factor too, but not the only one.

Most of the married-and-formerly-married holding better-paid and challenging jobs, perceive that a career has helped life's quality. That may not be true, however, for most women in the labor force, those who have combined with their marriage a lower-paid, routine, nonchallenging and nonprestigious white- or blue-collar job. These may feel differently. Even some of the women with highly paid successful careers occasionally feel differently, in part for reasons referred to by one survey respondent:

"While household help helps and a husband who helps shoulder family/home responsibilities is *essential,* there are *those* mornings on the way to the babysitter, and the car breaks down, and the housekeeper misses a day and you're having friends for dinner, and so on and on. You feel like chucking job, children, husband, and house. Instead what usually goes are personal interests and times to yourself with nothing to do. Price of sweet success!"

Help or Hindrance?

I have discoursed on how a career affects the quality of a married woman's life. How does marriage affect the career? About one-third of those asked perceive their careers to have been neither helped nor hurt. As for the other two-thirds, most of the married, a minority of the separated and divorced, feel that marriage *helped* their careers.

Marriage can *help* a career, particularly if the marriage is a satisfying one. A single woman prior to marriage may be concerned about her personal noncareer present and future as much as, or more than she is about her job and career. For her personal present she may be interested in enjoying life while she is young and unattached, without worrying too much about getting grimly serious about her career. For her personal future finding and marrying a prospective life's companion is of major importance, and that's where her thoughts and energy may be concentrated.

After marriage—the culmination of the search for a mate—the settling-down process, financial needs that come after marriage (for furniture, home, the couple's future), encouragement by the spouse—all may promote a concentration on the job and progress in the career.

One respondent comments on the connection between her marriage (her second), and success in her career.

"My second husband has been one of the primary reasons my career has done so well over the last three years. He is extremely supportive of my career and the time constraints that result from it. Household chores are done by whoever gets there first. It's usually him. He has always been an active stepfather to my daughter which has freed up my guilt of not being with her as much or having to travel for business. . . . I don't know how I could have achieved what I have if it weren't for my real partner in life."

The feeling that marriage helped holds for married women both with and without children, though understandably the enthusiasm of the former is more restrained. Offspring do require a diversion of energy and attention from mother's out-of-home occupation.

The separated and divorced have a different view of the situation than do the married. The majority of the separated and divorced believe the marriage did affect the career. Of those, however, most feel that marriage *hurt* it.

How did marriage *hurt* the formerly-married organization woman's career? The need to divide her attention and energies between home and career can certainly adversely affect a woman's job performance and thus career advancement. Marriage and family responsibilities, with or without children, can mean conflict with the time required to be spent on the job after normal hours or on weekends—whether on work itself; in company business meetings; at company social affairs; entertaining customers; at trade shows and conventions; or attending seminars and taking courses aimed at developing knowledge and skills needed for advancement. One observation is offered by an older and divorced woman: "Men usually expect unlimited overtime from women. They schedule meetings, etc. at closing time or Saturdays. They do not accept the fact that women have obligations at home."

Marriage can also curtail time spent on the job during normal hours if sickness of either children or husband requires absence from work.

Further, marriage can reduce the mental concentration focused on the job and the career during regular working hours or in off-hours, particularly if the marriage is a stressful one, and the spouse is less than fully supportive. Family needs interfere with travel requirements of the job, and with accepting promotions that require relocation to another city; and if a husband is transferred marriage may mean giving up a promising career with one organization to start over with a new job in a new location determined by where the husband is moved.

Let's look further at how marriage can hurt a career. *To climb far* up the corporate ladder a *man* all too often finds it necessary to be "married" to his job, his career. Long hours and hard work are expected. Very important, decried as it may be, *priority of attention* goes to the job, not to the family. The job comes first, and it can be all-consuming.

Children become the responsibility solely of the wife, who also must be supportive of the husband. At the same time the husband provides only limited support for the wife. If the job requires late night or weekend meetings, extensive entertainment of boring strangers, heavy travel and time away from home, or frequent relocation of residence, so be it. The wife and family are expected to go along with whatever is desirable to further the husband's career. If it should happen that the wife too has a career—that doesn't matter.

If a woman is *really ambitious* careerwise, with the added burden of male chauvinism and discrimination in the work place, not faced by a man, she must work even harder than a man. If she's married, and particularly if she has children, can she really give her *first priority to the job,* rather than to her family?

A husband's spouse may have been conditioned by society to expect to support the priority of her husband's career—and she will do it. The wife's spouse has not, and generally won't. Even a "liberated" nonchauvinistic husband is likely to place limits on how much priority he will allow to his wife's ambitions.

The woman thus has a sex-related limitation placed upon her. If she wants *high* career goals *plus* marriage, and especially if she wants children too, she's got real problems.

How does the boss feel about marriage and what it does to a woman's ability to progress? The male executives surveyed mostly claim to feel that marriage doesn't affect the quality of a woman's work or her career advancement one way or the other; one-third feel that it helps; not over 10 percent express the opinion that it interferes—*assuming the woman doesn't have children.* For the career woman *with* children, the majority of the men are convinced the family interferes both with doing a job well and with career advancement.

There are a number of reasons that an employer might object to hiring and promoting married women, and particularly those with children. The basic objection is the general priority accorded family needs (expected of the woman rather than the man of the household) over the needs of the employer. This shows up in absenteeism when someone in the family is sick, the reluctance to work after regular hours and during weekends when it becomes necessary, reluctance to participate in out-of-town travel, etc.

Home, Health, Children

The boss' belief that children interfere with a woman's job and career is evidenced by the answers to a direct question on this issue. It is also evidenced, however, by volunteered comments on open-ended questions regarding obstacles to a woman's getting ahead and on problems in working with career women.

The controller for a very large Southern California enterprise in pointing to obstacles to a woman's getting ahead in his company refers to "ingrained male attitudes, husbands want home to come first, with woman herself putting home first." A Memphis executive lists what he considers to be one of the most difficult problems in working with women: "Women's home priorities outweigh their job priorities—children, family crises, etc." A marketing vice president in Minneapolis comments that "infants at home" are an obstacle to a woman's progress in his organization. A Stamford, Connecticut executive thinks that among the greatest obstacles to a woman's advancement in his firm one should include an "ambivalent attitude towards career on one hand and marriage/family on the other; inability to effectively sort out personal goals/priorities."

Other comments by men on problems working with women include: "outside demands on their time (homemaking, children, shopping, etc.);" "their preoccupation with 'home life;' " and "lack of time to devote to business problems outside of normal office hours."

An electrical engineer, a single woman in her twenties, similarly considers "prejudice that she will marry and have children and be undependable, i.e., subjugate job to her 'family responsibilities' " is indeed a strong obstacle to promotion even for one who is not married, but some day might be.

A very successful procurement manager for a large construction firm, a woman, claims "I would not have been able to accomplish this position with children. Not that many hours in a day!"

A female vice president of a Denver bank points to the serious handicap faced by women "if they have children and sitter problems so they can't be with peers occasionally after work, available to go out with customers, etc."

Yet according to a corporate director of government affairs, a married woman in her thirties with children, "careers, children, and marriage can mix in a harmonious blend if all players understand the rules at the beginning of the relationship. There are constant trade-offs and everyone must be willing to compromise."

Along lines not dissimilar a district manager in Indianapolis, a single woman in her thirties, is irritated with "women who want a career, but who expect interference from traditional family responsibilities to be accepted and ignored in selection of promotional candidates or business performance evaluations, especially when they refuse to make arrangements to reduce interference.''

A married personnel recruiter with children, in her thirties, also declaims: "If you have a job—you should make arrangements for your children to be cared for when well or sick. Your salary is being paid for the work you do, not to take care of your children.

"If I could not be sure my two children were well taken care of, or if they were hurting from my working—I would quit—they and my husband are *top* priorities to me. Too many women are thrown into the business world with the idea if a firm hires them, they are hiring the children, and any problems that come with them.

"You can't make a profit doing that.

"If you organize you can accomplish everything and still work a full-time job.'' (Superwoman?)

From the employer's viewpoint a married woman with children is less likely to be willing to travel than a woman without children; and both are less likely to travel willingly than an unmarried woman. Travel is an important factor, and its importance increases with career advancement.

The following comment by a career woman illustrates another aspect: "My superior hates for me to travel under less than ideal conditions, as I am more 'subject' to crime and/or injury than male counterparts. He knows I am more experienced and adept in travel situations than he; but—'What do I tell your husband if you don't come home?' ''

Geographic location poses another problem for the employer of married women. An organization's interests may dictate the relocation of professional personnel or experienced managers from places where they can be spared or readily replaced to places where they are needed. Moreover, a capable person very often gets transferred from a staff position in one city to a line position in another, or from a smaller branch in one area to a larger one elsewhere—as part of a process of training, broadening, and upgrading. Further, promotions occur in the form of transfers to places where vacancies which represent promotions occur. In any case, transfers are part of progress in a career.

Yet married career women generally, by a considerable margin, are more likely to decline than to accept transfers. The tendency to decline is lowest among those with the best jobs among the women surveyed. Nevertheless, a majority of even those with the best jobs claim to have declined promotions offered them which involved a move to another city; and expect to decline such offers in the future.

The married woman may not relocate for fear of disrupting her husband's career. In the words of the executive vice president of a Portland, Oregon corporation: "Because of jobs their husbands hold they often limit their promotion opportunities as they cannot take a transfer to another city." Even if the husband agrees to move, it may be with reluctance, which places strain on the marriage. If there are children, disruption of their schooling and lives is a further consideration. Moreover, social and community ties, friends and relatives, and the security of familiarity with the present surroundings, all play a part in the reluctance of women to move.

Ties similar to those for women make men also reluctant to move, but less so. A man enters a career *expecting* to relocate from time to time if he is going to progress. If he is married, his wife will expect to follow him, even if she has her own career—though if a married woman is offered a promotion in another city the husband in most cases won't follow her.

The knowledge that most will decline later transfers discourages an employer from training and promoting married women. The senior vice president of a Baltimore concern believes the problem of transfers is one of the greatest of the obstacles to female upward movement in his company. He complains of the "husband and family who stop a promotable because they don't want to move." As another male executive expresses it, there is an "inability to move to where promotions are available."

The employer has another fear in dealing with the married woman—the possible impermanence of the woman's employment. Impermanence may arise from transfer of a husband and the likelihood that the wife will then quit to follow her husband. It may also arise from the ever-present possibility that a married woman will decide to quit in order to have children or to stay home. Even an unmarried woman may get married, with the accompanying risks for the employer. See Chapter 11 for a general discussion and comments on the perceptions of the male executive relative to the impermanence of career women.

What is the effect of the career on the married woman? The effect on the quality of life has already been discussed. So has the possible effect on the numbers of women who will have children. Carrying on two careers, one in business and one in the home (marriage) can be a hassle. Does the combination have an effect on a woman's health? A substantial portion of those queried don't think so or don't know. Of the 60 percent among those surveyed who believe it does, the majority of the women with children, by a considerable margin, believe health has been hurt, not helped, by the combination. This is true for all income groups.

Among the women who believe health has been affected, the "two-careers" life mode is perceived mostly as *harmful* to health by both those without as well as those with children—except by the childless women with the best jobs, those earning $35,000 or more annually. The latter's voting margin is a little in favor of *helped* rather than *hurt* on health. Presumably money and a standard of living, an absorbing challenge and interest in the job, feeling important on the job and feeling good about one's success, counteract the stress of the marriage-career combination, and promote the perception or reality of a beneficial effect on health.

For the separated and divorced the percentage of women who feel their health has been adversely affected by the combination of marriage and career is just a little more than for those who are married, but the difference is not significant.

As a matter of interest, regardless of what our survey seems to show as to health and work outside the home, it should be pointed out that a 1983 analysis of a federal health survey apparently indicates that "working women have a higher sense of well-being, see doctors less often and have fewer emotional problems than their stay-at-home counterparts." (*Wall Street Journal,* Oct. 13, 1983, p. 1).

What about the effect of a career on the marriage itself? A career can help if it provides a second income that permits a standard of living not possible without it. If it gives a woman a feeling of pride and self-respect, and her husband a sense of admiration for his wife's accomplishments, her career helps the marriage. An improved quality of life for the woman too can affect her personality. A spouse happy with herself is more companionable and lovable than an unhappy one.

On the whole, more of the women surveyed claimed the career helped than claimed it hurt their marriage. There are considerable differences, however, in the perceptions of different groups. The *now-married woman* by a comfortable margin feels her marriage has been *helped* by her career. The *woman now separated or divorced* by a considerably wider margin perceives that the pursuit of a career *hurt* her marriage.

Children and income are factors influencing perceptions. Among women earning at least $35,000 annually, those married with children under eighteen feel by a considerable margin that the career helped the marriage. For the married earning less than $35,000, with children, the number claiming the marriage has been helped is only about the same as the number claiming it has been hurt. For both income groups, married women *without* children feel by a wide margin that the marriage benefited from the career.

While a career can help a marriage it can also hurt. The diversion of a woman's time and attention, effort, support, and priorities from children, and/or a spouse, from home to enhancing the profits of the Megabucks Corporation, may be resented by her marriage partner. So may childbearing delayed, or altogether sidetracked to pursue a career.

The continual pressures of two jobs can adversely affect personality as well as health, disadvantageously for the marriage. Further, relations with a husband can be strained by the wife's job requirements—travel, for example, and as part of the job, entertaining men.

Travel doesn't help the family relationship. One young married career woman in her thirties, without children, travels frequently and as a result comments that she has "less contact with husband . . . are growing apart and both of us have 'outside interests' (mutually undiscussed)—not best of situations."

Again, nearly half the women questioned entertain men at least somewhat, such as at lunch or dinner or the theatre, as part of the job. To a fair chunk of this half who entertain, that presents some social and even some sexual difficulties. The entertaining doesn't strengthen the marriage.

After-hours or out-of-town meetings (part of the job) which include both men and women, are resented considerably by the wives of the men present. They're also resented by the husbands of the women present. Even in regard simply to after-hours work by the woman, a husband may feel resentful. Quoting from one career woman: "If my husband must work late I am made to feel reverence. If I must work late I am made to feel guilt."

If successful in her job a woman may be offered a promotion involving a move to another city. If the career gets to mean a great deal to the wife there is a temptation to accept. Even if she declines, as is likely, the result may be strain within the family as well as with her boss.

The pressures of a "two-careers" life style is likely to force a husband with a macho self-image unwillingly to compromise with that image and help with the household chores. Despite the reasonableness of sharing those chores, 27 percent of the spouses of the organization women surveyed don't; for them the chores remain mostly the woman's.

Combining a career and marriage can be hard on a woman, and can affect adversely both health, already discussed, and the irritability index of the woman. Neither effect helps a marriage. There is a stress factor, and interestingly, a full 20 percent of the organization women surveyed admit that increase in job stress with career advancement is likely to deter them from seeking additional promotions in the future.

The following is illuminating. The percentages represent the proportions of all the women surveyed, married and not married, who believe the listed situations would create a significant problem for most career women.

	Percent
Women often traveling out of town; longer than three days at a time	73
Husband working for same employer as wife	71
Bringing at-work problems into the home	66
Earnings of woman exceeding husband's	64
Woman often traveling out of town: 2 or 3 days at a time	42

Except for the last item, for all situations a majority of the married, of the separated or divorced, and of the single indicated their belief that a problem would exist.

Earnings exceeding the husband's is fourth on the list of five problem situations overall. It is noted, however, that for the separated and divorced that question of earnings is the most critical one—first on their list.

Of the married women we surveyed, 60 percent earn more than their husbands and 13 percent work for the same employer as the husband. If necessary to move to another city to advance their careers, 31 percent of the women would do so; only 20 percent claim they would not because of the husband's career; and 49 percent claim they would not, but professedly for reasons other than the husband's career.

What happens if a wife is successful in her career? The husband may resent it, his macho self-image deteriorate, and animosity develop. The wife may lose her respect for the husband's abilities if she herself does better in a career. She may gain a sense of her own worth and financial independence—the former lack of which may have kept her tied to an unhappy marriage, or to one not as happy as she thinks another way of life could be.

Another possibility is that she could gain an exaggerated idea of her own worth that makes her difficult to live with; or, simply a valid one, which her husband finds too threatening to his own ego.

A career may lessen the personal dependence of a wife on her husband. It provides her separate contacts with others on whom she can lean for support (associates, new friends, mentors—male and female). There is a chance to develop a spirit of independence by virtue of a separate income of course, but also by virtue of experience in activities and decision making on her own, apart from her husband.

The career and career-related work, travel, entertaining, and social activities lead to acquaintance with many men other than her husband. This opens the door for comparisons adverse to her husband, and widens the opportunities for new sex interests too.

To summarize, there is little doubt that for many marriages a career in the business world is beneficial. There is also little doubt that for many, heavy emphasis on a career is detrimental, particularly when there are children. For the woman who feels she would like to have both marriage and an exceptional career, this raises complex questions. For the woman who also wants children the complications are compounded.

But if the second income is needed the wife's career is a necessity.

Whether because of the money or otherwise, it is also true that for the great majority of the organization women studied, married or divorced, with or without children, the career seems to raise the quality of life. That's important too!

11

Sex, Sexual Overtones, and Personal Problems

Sex and sexual overtones are present in the business organization, as they are elsewhere. Their existence is inevitable in a work setting which includes both men and women.

There is, as a division manager of a Georgia corporation puts it, the "omnipresence of sex/sexuality in an environment which pretends it doesn't exist or is irrelevant." The financial officer of a major Los Angeles enterprise notes that "the sexual effects still get in the way occasionally even in an enlightened atmosphere, i.e., there is a difference between male and female." And a woman vice president of a New England insurance company, in her thirties, considers as an obstacle she faces in trying to get ahead in her company "the man who can't get over the fact that I am a female, yet won't admit it even to himself—the 'purported' liberated man who's really very hung up on sex and is very conscious of a woman's sex."

"They Look Instead of Listen"

A female personnel manager in California complains that the men in her company "see me as a female first—normally takes a couple of meetings before they listen instead of look." Other career women lament that "it is difficult to make men look at a woman executive as an executive, not as a woman;" that the "sex problem is and always will be present—there is always tension;" and that "I'm the first to be noticed in a meeting—inability to sit back and watch the interchange flow; always on the firing line; ideas have to be better in general than men's so that my mind gets dealt with rather than my sexuality." Then too there is the woman who finds herself "worrying about crossing my legs at meetings" even while discussing vexatious managerial problems.

Sex is indeed alive and well in the career world. Survey participants, men and women, were asked about the effects.

To begin with, good looks and a slender figure generally have been considered helpful to a woman and few of the management women or male bosses surveyed consider them as such, to be without advantage. Also, don't looks and slenderness connote confidence and efficacy? The overweight often appear depressed and slow-moving, less alert and alacritous, less up on things since thin is in. The one disadvantage of course is possible resentment by other women. A corporate industrial relations manager, a young woman in her thirties, confesses to problems in dealing with resentful female subordinates who believe she got her position on the basis of looks.

Physical presence is helpful. Accenting sex unduly, however, is believed by most to be hurtful, and carried too far may be fatal to a woman's career in her company. Dressing seductively is considered by the great majority of both sexes queried to be definitely disadvantageous. The male president of a Northern California firm's advice: "Look like a business person—not a movie star."

Even dressing sexily just occasionally is considered to be either without advantage or actually disadvantageous. In the words of a young single, under thirty, highly-paid career woman, a New York executive: "NEVER! A good silk dress is the limit, and then only for special celebration dinners."

A minority, one-fourth of the women and one-third of the executives, think there *is* an advantage in occasional display; but few of these consider it more than minor.

Dressing casually on occasion may be permissible, but as a regular thing is of no advantage in the eyes of the great majority of the men and women, and most of these believe it produces a negative effect.

When it comes to women's clothes, the uniform of the business organization is prescribed by the senior vice president of a San Francisco corporation, a man, "dress nicely, but conservatively" and by the advertising director of a Texas clothing chain, a woman, "conservative suits, shirts, and shoes."

Using Sex

What about occasional flirting? The preponderance of both men and women hold it to be either of no advantage, or harmful. With men who don't like it, or with men who like it but not at the wrong time, flirting can be annoying. It can be especially annoying to other observing women—who may have memories and carry knives. One young professional refers to "flirting, acting helpless, trying to get male employees' 'sexual interests' " as the most irritating of the problems she encounters in dealing with women in the work place. Another agrees she strongly dislikes "women who encourage men by flirting in the office."

How often does flirting actually take place? Most of the women and the executives surveyed believe it occurs occasionally. A few of the women, almost none of the men, claim it happens often. The women are more aware of it than are the men in top management, their bosses; or more readily admit to its existence (perhaps because they resent its use by other women as a substitute for professional ability?). Possibly too, career women, at lower echelons, see it (or use it) more often than do the male executives, those surveyed, in their more rarefied atmosphere at the top.

Women may have several objectives in flirting: the attraction of a potential mate (whether permanent or fleeting); the pleasure of confirming their sexual attractiveness; to overcome job deficiencies and career restrictions imposed by limited competence; and to obtain favors.

A woman's use of her sexuality for gain in an organization is of concern to the men who run that organization. In noting the most important factor(s), in addition to performance, for a woman wanting to get ahead in their companies, male executives spell out, and we quote some examples, the "ability to work with others, able to avoid male/female stuff;" "being able to function without being 'special;' " "the ability to relate to fellow workers as an employee—not as a woman;" the "suppression of sexuality in career matters;" "reduce focus on womanhood;" and "her ability to gain the respect of her peers and her supervisors by knowledge and performance—unrelated to or unaffected by her sex."

There is a strong impression from the many comments received from the male bosses surveyed that the use by women of their sexuality to make up for incompetence, to obtain advancement, and to get favored treatment is *greatly* resented. So is the expectation or any implied expectation by women of preferred treatment as compared to men, merely because they are women, even without blunt exploitation of sexuality.

A corporate treasurer in California criticizes the "use of their sexual attractiveness to overcome technical incompetence. Use of their need for protection as a female." Another executive asserts that "relying on sexual attraction to carry her beyond her job capabilities/performance" is *not* the way a woman is going to advance in his company. A New York vice president, a woman, likewise is irritated by "women who are not well qualified, yet think they are 'owed' a position or advancement simply because they're women. There aren't many in my firm currently." "Watching some women use their sex to try to get ahead" similarly irks a female personnel professional in San Francisco.

The president of a Georgia enterprise believes that in his firm, a woman in "trying to use her femininity to get preferential treatment," only succeeds in creating an obstacle to her further advancement. A Delaware vice president expresses the same sentiment in respect to women "expecting preferential treatment/seeking favors" in his company.

A corporate vice president in Kansas City confirms a perception that some women want special favors: ". . . wanting to be treated equal except in instances where they want special favors because they're women." Another man, a St. Paul financial officer, observes of women: "Some feel the need to be treated more gently than men, but do expect all the benefits of the job—in other words—not always willing to pay the full price." The male personnel director of a major Tulsa corporation cites a "tendency for some women professionals to seem to desire to be treated [both] as women and as professionals—leading at times to role confusion." A young female engineer, under thirty, in the mining industry, appears to express somewhat the same thought: "Putting up with their remarks. They make me feel defensive about working in a 'man's' world and more defensive still wanting to be treated like a woman. *I want both*" [underscoring is the author's].

Harassment

Men may feel women use their sexuality unfairly, or unfairly expect priority in advancement and special treatment because they are women. Women, on the other hand, have some sex-related complaints too, and they are widespread. They face verbal harassment in the way men address them; and in the language, remarks, and jokes with which they are at times deliberately showered.

The chief financial officer of a Southern California retail chain, a woman in her thirties, doesn't relish "being addressed as 'doll,' 'hon,' 'dear,' etc." Nor does an Indianapolis controller in her forties like "men who use phrases such as 'dear,' etc., in talking to women, or men who are 'touchers.' " A young St. Paul manager, still in her twenties, but highly paid and with over 20 men and women reporting to her, resents "having them call me 'kid' or 'sweetheart.' " A young research engineer in Northern California is irked that "I am patronized at times, teased constantly, and told I'm 'cute' when I'm angry and frustrated."

There are other "little things" like the manager of purchasing services who finds "it's irritating to win a professional award and be kissed instead of just handshaked."

More irritating than manner of address is the male peers'

language, dirty jokes, and innuendo. In reply to "What I consider to be the most difficult, irritating, frustrating and/or distasteful problem(s) for me as a woman working with men," organization women refer time and again to foul language. While such language occurs in social settings, it is somehow more "threatening" in a business environment where the woman is a "captive audience" and exposed to it from people with whom she is continually in a work relationship—or so it seems from the number of comments made and their intensity.

Thus a San Francisco woman is angered by " 'dirty mouths' who obtain gratification by shocking females with their lewd remarks; and condescension." A Memphis management information specialist in her twenties objects to peer males "telling jokes that are extremely filthy, only to embarrass me. (Another problem—or difficulty—is that some jokes—mildly dirty ones—are funny to me, but should I laugh?)"

As a Minnesota accounting department manager in her thirties analyzes it, "men over-react. Either they try so hard to not say 'bad' words or dirty stories because of me, which causes discomfort, or they go the other way and make little jokes highlighting the discomfort of me being a woman." And the controller of a smaller Northern California firm, in her forties, is irritated with men in her company "grouping women in generalities. Example: All women are grouchy once a month."

Many female respondents voice intense dislike for the sexual innuendos to which they are subjected by the men they work with. These range from the relatively innocuous "good old boys insisting that my work has a 'woman's touch' " to "they comment on how 'sexy' a new secretary is" to "What does your husband think of . . . " to "sexual overtones by a boss . . . "

Some further survey excerpts suggest that men "have difficulty getting past the need to be attractive to working women" and "that most all think they are Burt Reynolds and would love to make it with them [women]."

One of the occupational hazards faced by the career woman is described by a manager of a Texas company, a married woman in her forties who hates "attending an out-of-town meeting with a majority of men also attending who get carried away with drinking and telling embarrassing jokes or stories;" a younger Memphis analyst, in her twenties and single, similarly dislikes the necessity of "socializing with intoxicated male superiors."

Another occupational hazard is the resentment of the managerial woman by her subordinates who take it for granted that, in the words of a personnel vice president, a married woman in her thirties, "I got where I am by 'sleeping with the boss.' " The vice president of a clothing chain also faces snide subordinates: "They assume you are sleeping with someone or have in the past in order to achieve a vice presidential level job." An engineer complains of the women she works with: "They seem to resent me more than the men. They don't believe you can have just a 'working' relationship [with the men]." Referring to subordinates, another choice excerpt from a female respondent: "[They] think you're trying to get into the boss' pants."

And an executive from Minnesota, a man in his thirties, ruefully acknowledges a hazard: "If one works well with women executives' suspicions are raised."

"Getting Involved"

Half the career women and a substantial number of the bosses express the opinion that affairs with the boss or other influential males occur occasionally in their organizations. Affairs with other males, noninfluential ones, are a bit more common; most of the women and even half the men admit these happen from time to time. Possibly sex for love, with noninfluential males, is more common than sex for pure advantage, or under duress, with the boss. It is intriguing to note that the career women queried are either more sensitive to, or open in admitting, or more desirous of pointing out the occurrence in their firms of sexual intimacy, than are the men surveyed.

A young career woman offers an insight into intra-company affairs in a smaller firm in Texas: "I can handle the men, but not the woman I work for. She resents me because before I came along, she was the only woman. She has slept with three-fourths of the men and she usually gets her way with them. I feel that as long as she is my boss I will not be given any chances to move up unless I play up to the men—which I will not do.''

The general manager of a large division of a St. Louis conglomerate sums it up on ''. . . dealing with sexual attraction in a business environment. Man is . . . a rational animal, but . . . as with any animal, when a male and female are placed together for any period of time biology is bound to rear its ugly head. To indulge those urges can be awkward, counterproductive and disruptive later on. Wives know this, husbands know it, and Phil Donahue knows it. This also makes things a little hot at home and with good reason. It's a real problem and I'm not sure if anything can ever be done about it—except ignore it—to the extent possible.''

Very few of the men and very few of the women queried see any advantage to be gained in affairs with the boss or other influential males—despite the young woman from the smaller firm in Texas. The great preponderance of both men and women feel such affairs are disadvantageous to the career woman.

A woman manager in Dallas considers the greatest obstacle to a woman's getting ahead in her company: "Getting involved personally with men you work with, in social situations, or on the job;" to which another woman adds: "any sort of sexual problems with any men in the company." An affair often will end with at least one party leaving the company.

The man in most cases is considered to be more valuable to the company than is the woman, in an office affair. Hence it is the woman who most often is likely to have to leave her job.

Many organizations have a tough rule even for the males who get themselves involved (with intra-company females). This toughness applies also to the women. In one situation the man heading a chain of women's clothing stores had been highly successful in increasing sales volume and profits. Rumor had it he was destined for higher things in the parent organization which owned the chain. But he did promote one woman in his chain with greater rapidity and to a higher position than would normally be expected for a subordinate with good, but nevertheless limited abilities.

Yes—he was having an affair! When the news finally got through to parent headquarters, his severance from the chain was quick and complete, despite the excellent performance of the chain he headed. And of course, the woman left too.

A majority of the women surveyed claim that sexual harassment of career women occurs on the job, verbally, by touching, and in the form of proposed (at least semiseriously) intimacy—all three—in their companies. Of this majority, most claim the harassment occurs "occasionally".

As to the men surveyed, a lesser majority, but still well over half, indicate that verbal harassment occurs from time to time, and about half also agree that touching and proposed intimacy occur at least once in a while. A fair number of the women and a few of the men venture the opinion that the three forms of harassment occur often.

Does sexual harassment of managerial women go as far as actual intimacy? Fully 22 percent of the women surveyed believe it does, more than rarely, though only 1 percent claim it occurs often. Of the males, 17 percent believe harassment goes that far at least occasionally, but again only 1 percent claim it occurs often.

That sexual harassment is a problem is underscored by the numerous references to it from women surveyed—"sexual harassment;" "sexual advances and feelings that women are inferior;" "sexual advances (totally unwanted);" "sexual pressure, men who want to dominate women;" and more mildly, "men who are 'touchers;' " and "physical gestures."

One woman worries about "always standing possibility of having to refuse male approach and suffering potential downgrading of work and future due to such refusal." Another, the office manager of a textile firm in the East, married and in her thirties, sums up her opinion: "I think the majority of women in career fields would feel that sexual harassment would be the most difficult [problem for a woman, as a woman working with men]."

One executive woman is quoted in *The Wall Street Journal*[11] as saying: "It's very hard to parry a proposition skillfully. It always comes across as a shock. . . . Many women try to laugh off advances, afraid to anger a boss or a client. But more are taking a direct approach. . . . 'You and I are going to be working together, and I don't want anything to get in the way of our good working relationship.' I don't smile when I say that.''

A young engineer in Northern California had to quit her job because of demands for sex by her supervisor. She got another position and later had the satisfaction of learning that the man she had formerly reported to had been fired. The supervisor's boss had learned about a pattern of such sex demands by that supervisor, something which company policy could not tolerate.

Many women are reluctant to report the occurrence of sexual harassment, for reasons summed up by one female in the following, quoted by Eliza Collins and Timothy Blodgett in the *Harvard Business Review*[20]: ''(1) Don't think they'll be believed; (2) will be punished by smaller raises or cruddy jobs; (3) will be ostracized by male and female employees; (4) will be accused of inviting the advance; (5) have guilt feelings that perhaps it was invited subconsciously; (6) fear publicity; (7) are unsure exactly what is harassment and what is just interaction of people.''

Do the managerial and professional women and staff specialists being discussed harass men, or at least try to make use of sexual connotations or sex on the job? Certainly by the way they dress and by appeals to male gallantry or protectiveness they do. The majority of the male executives, and even more so the majority of the organization women queried, believe some women make use of these approaches occasionally; some 7 to 10 percent of the women and 3 to 4 percent of the men believe the techniques are used often. More than half the females and almost half the males believe career women occasionally use sexual verbal innuendo on the job.

As to intimacy, almost one-third of the women believe that career women in their firms occasionally propose intimacy to men in their firms, at least semiseriously, and very nearly as many believe the women sometimes seek or encourage actual intimacy. Fewer, but nevertheless a substantial number of the male executives believe these sexual advances occur more than rarely.

Complaints from career women about ''the most difficult, irritating, frustrating and/or distasteful problem(s) for me as a woman working with other women are—"Innuendos with male co-workers;" "women who use men sexually to get ahead;" and one by a married New York woman still in her twenties, but a highly-paid vice president of her firm: "Women who undermine career women in general by flamboyance plus affairs with business associates. The two are not unrelated and make no mistake, most men recognize the difference between the two types of 'business women.'"

Because they are female, organization women sometimes face other difficulties in the work environment. These relate to socializing with their male colleagues, travel, entertaining men as part of the job (especially if the job is in sales), transfers and promotions which involve moving to another city, and the perception by male bosses that the woman is an impermanent employee.

Most organization women do socialize on the job (lunch, etc.) at least somewhat with male colleagues. Off the job most socialize "not much" with the same colleagues. Thus 43 percent of the women queried claim that on the job they socialize with their male counterparts "somewhat", another 30 percent claim "a lot," and only 27 percent claim "not much." Off the job, 26 percent claim "some" socializing, only 6 percent "a lot," and fully 68 percent claim "not much."

As the income of the organization woman goes up the amount of socializing with male colleagues increases considerably on the job, but not markedly off the job. As would be expected, the younger women socialize with male associates to a greater extent than do the older women, both on and off the job.

There is no significant difference between the married and the unmarried in socializing on the job. Off the job, however, the married socialize with the men a bit more than do the unmarried, though for both married and unmarried, not nearly as much as on the job.

Going Places

Travel, as we have noted, can be a major factor in the progress of a woman in her organization. As one climbs the corporate ladder its importance increases. Fully one-fourth of the women earning $35,000 and more annually claim to travel "a lot" on the job. Over half travel "occasionally." Only 20 percent of the $35,000-and-over group claim "little or none." For those earning less than $35,000 per year only 10 percent travel a lot, 45 percent occasionally, and 45 percent little or none. For all income groups, travel is generally alone, but often with colleagues, mostly male.

For most of the women travel presents little difficulty on account of being a woman. But for over one-third of those who do travel it presents some; considerably less for those in higher income groups. Perhaps this is in part because higher-income women travel more frequently and have therefore adjusted better; or perhaps the higher-income women are simply women who can more aggressively cope.

The frequency of travel is roughly the same for the married and the unmarried. See Chapter 10 on travel and the married woman. The older women surveyed do more traveling than do the younger ones, on average. As would be expected, however, difficulties are faced more frequently by the younger than by the older travelers.

As part of the job, two-thirds of the organization women earning at least $35,000 annually entertain men "somewhat" or "a lot" (such as at lunch or dinner or at the theater). Close to a quarter of all the women in this income bracket entertain men a lot. For those earning less the corresponding figures are 30 percent "somewhat" or "a lot;" and 7 percent, "a lot."

For those who do entertain as part of the job, does this present difficulties?—Socially? Yes, somewhat, for about 35 percent (about 25 percent for those earning at least $35,000 annually, considerably more for those earning less); and a lot for 3 to 4 percent. Sexually? Yes, somewhat, for about 30 percent (about 25 percent for both those earning at least $35,000 and those earning $25,000 to $35,000 annually; considerably more for those earning less); and a lot for 3 to 4 percent of the women surveyed. As would be expected, social and sexual difficulties in entertaining are less for the older women than for the younger.

Upward progress in a career often involves a transfer or

change of job to another city. Such a move is especially difficult for those who are married, as discussed in Chapter 11; it's also difficult for the unmarried.

Of the organization women surveyed 26 percent have been offered promotion(s) involving a move to another city. Of those earning at least $35,000 annually 38 percent have received such offers. Of those earning $25,000 to $35,000 per year 20 percent have received offers. For those earning less than $25,000 the figure is 11 percent. Roughly 2 of 5 women overall have accepted promotion(s) involving a move; the other 3 of 5 have not. The tendency to decline is least for those with the best jobs. Just under one-third of the married as compared with about half of the unmarried have accepted.

Impermanence

Employers fear the possible impermanence of a woman's employment. Male executives are highly skeptical about the likelihood of a woman remaining with the organization for many years. This affects the degree to which a firm is likely to want to push for the promotion of a female. If a woman is not going to remain with the company for a long period of time, why invest in training and developing her, through a series of promotions, for the more important positions in the firm?

In the words of an older company executive, a male, from Memphis: "Management is unsure about the retention of women—will she leave for non-job-related reasons (husband transferred, children's needs, lack of need to work after family is economically stable—house paid for, etc.) . . . women's home priorities outweigh their job priorities . . . "

And if a woman is single, will she marry and quit later for the same non-job-related reasons?

The vice president of a leading Michigan firm notes that in his opinion, particularly "a woman with a family (especially younger children) is often suspect concerning dedication and longevity."

In reply to a survey question: "The proportion of all, line and staff, who will continue with a full-time career until at least the age of sixty,'' 55 percent of the male executives surveyed expressed the opinion that at least half the career women will not. Only 21 percent of the men believe as many as 80 percent of the women will.

Further, in reply to: ''I plan to continue with a full-time career in either my present or another organization until at least the age of sixty,'' only 69 percent of career women themselves, those surveyed, indicated they would; and that despite the fact that close to half the women queried were already age forty or more and thus to some extent by then ''locked in'' to continuing work until sixty. Of the women 20 percent claim they plan to continue working, but with time off—12 percent for children, 8 percent for other reasons; 2 percent do not expect to work continually to age sixty; 9 percent don't know. It is of course the younger women who plan to take time off for children. This includes an estimated close to half of those under age thirty-five.

If financial considerations were unimportant would the organization women keep on with their careers? Seventy-seven percent claim they would, 6 percent claim they would not, and 17 percent aren't sure. (The same question was not asked of the organization males surveyed).

The male executive vice president of a New York-based conglomerate points to another problem related to the perceived impermanence of the female employee. It is job-hopping by an ambitious woman who, as she gains experience, works her way up the ladder of success by continual moves from one company to another (perhaps companies which want qualified managerial women to fill ''affirmative action'' needs?). Quoting him on this, the possibility of a woman's ''selling of reputation and experience to next highest bidder'' leads to a conclusion that she's ''not worth training for short tenure.''

12

Your Legal Rights

How Title VII Works

If a woman has been discriminated against on her job, or in applying for a job, because of her sex, she has certain legal rights. Title VII of the Civil Rights Act of 1964, as amended in 1972, prohibits discrimination in employment as to hiring, dismissal, compensation, terms, conditions, privileges of employment, and promotion. It makes it illegal to discriminate on the basis of race, color, religion, sex, or national origin. Title VII applies, since 1972, to employers of 15 or more, "engaged in an industry affecting commerce." It also applies to employment agencies, in referring applicants to prospective jobs; to labor organizations, and to all local, state, and federal governmental units. Present or former employees, apprentices, union members, and applicants for employment, apprenticeships, and union membership can bring action under Title VII. Sex discrimination is permitted where a bona fide occupational qualification makes it reasonably necessary to discriminate for the normal operation of a specific business.

The 1972 amendments to the 1964 Act gives the Equal Employment Opportunity Commission the power to sue in the agency's name on behalf of those discriminated against. The Act also permits the courts to order the payment of attorney's fees as part of an award for damages suffered by one who has been discriminated against. Also, Section 704 of Title VII provides that "it shall be unlawful employment practice for an employer to discriminate against any of his employees . . . because [the employee] has opposed any practice made an unlawful employment practice by this title, or because [the employee] has made a charge, testified, assisted, or participated in any manner in an investigation, proceeding, or hearing under this title."

Where persons of equal qualifications are not given equal employment opportunities and treatment, irrespective of sex, and without a business justification, discrimination exists. Thus, refusing employment applications from women with preschool-age children, but accepting such applications from men with preschool-age children, has been held to be illegal by the U.S. Supreme Court.

One of the crudest forms of discrimination is segregation of jobs by sex. Only men are hired for "men's" jobs and only women for "women's" jobs. Employers can present as a defense a bona fide occupational need for a male in a specific "men's" job or for females in a specific "women's" job. The courts have tended to allow this defense, however, only where the need to limit a job to one sex appears to be conclusive, where the *essence* of a business operation will be undermined by not hiring all or nearly all employees holding that job from one sex only. Because the courts have been restrictive in their allowance of occupational need as justification for sex discrimination we do now have female firefighters and police, and male airline stewards.

A less open form of job segregation by sex involves the use of physical requirements such as height, weight, and strength requirements that exceed what a job really demands, and where job needs can reasonably be tailored to avoid excessive physical requirements. Excessive physical requirements can eliminate many or most women from the jobs for which those requirements are specified.

Physical specifications constitute practices which have an unequal impact on the female and the male. Unequal impact practices are those which on the surface are impartial in their treatment of different groups, yet are discriminatory in their impact. Height requirements, for example, don't eliminate women from a job "because they are women," but they do in fact affect women more adversely than they do men. It has been argued that they are justified by business or occupational necessity. As indicated, however, courts have tended to allow defense on this basis only where the need is decisive.

The fact that a sex-discriminatory requirement for selection of employees is job-related does not necessarily avoid a charge of sex discrimination. If alternative requirements which will not discriminate by gender would serve the requirements of the work to be done, such alternatives may be mandated by the courts.

Overt proof of discriminatory motive in cases involving segregation of jobs by sex, or in cases of unequal impact of job specifications on men and women, is not necessarily required. The very fact of segregation by sex and of impact differences may be sufficient to infer discriminatory motives. Statistical breakdowns of the relevant populations in the geographic area of employment and correspondingly of employees holding the various jobs in a firm, provide a commonly used tool to show inequality in job selection or in the impact of supposedly "gender-neutral" job requirements.

"Disparate treatment" cases are those where an employer, despite professed policy or practice, does in fact treat one or more women less favorably than men as to promotion, pay, or conditions of work, etc. In disparate treatment cases employer *intent* to discriminate on account of gender must be proved. To some degree intent may be inferred from the facts of a situation, but these of themselves may not be sufficient to *prove* intent. Employers can very often come up with apparently rational and nondiscriminatory reasons, real or not, for disparate treatment, especially where a case involves only one woman as the object of discrimination.

But discriminatory employment practices usually affect many persons, not just one solitary individual. Title VII consequently allows discrimination lawsuits to be brought by one or more individuals on behalf of a class of individuals. Thus a woman who has been discriminated against may sue her employer, not only for herself, but for all other women who are discriminated against by the employer. One lawsuit indeed can cover a multiplicity of an employer's discriminatory practices, inclusive of recruiting, hiring, assignment of work, employment terms and conditions, and promotions. Proving, via statistical analysis, discrimination against a class may be easier than proving discrimination against one individual, particularly in cases of disparate treatment. Discriminatory treatment of an *individual* can be denied on the ground that discharge or lack of promotion, etc. was the result of the individual's on-the-job deficiencies, not discrimination. Denial is more difficult where a *group* or *class* has been discriminated against.

The law holds that an employer has an obligation to undertake "affirmative action" to correct inequality where women have been discriminated against and kept out of "men's jobs," for example jobs in management or specific professional or specialist positions, in a firm. The employer is required therefore, where appropriate, to take specific action to ensure that an adequate number of women are recruited for all jobs, including managerial and professional jobs, that training programs and apprenticeships are filled by women as well as men, that promotional opportunities are available to women, etc.

To a degree the affirmative action programs developed by employers to meet their governmental requirements constitute a "quota" system. The implied or express need to fill job "quotas" set up for women to show that a company is not discriminating has meant in many cases that women have actually had preference over men in filling vacancies and in being selected for promotions. Indeed, of the women I surveyed, 21 percent admitted that in addition to ability and performance, affirmative action was a significant factor in their promotion to or being hired into their present job. I suspect the figure would be higher, but for a natural reluctance to attribute promotion to government-inspired "quotas." And if redressing the past is to be expedited, then perhaps quota-inspired preferences constitute one tool for doing so.

Where layoffs or promotions or work assignments are tied to

seniority systems women often will be discriminated against. Persons with the highest seniority will get preference. Since women are often the ones with least seniority, particularly in filling jobs which previously were filled altogether or almost altogether by men, they will to that degree suffer. Although a bona fide seniority system is allowed to continue to operate under Title VII a seniority system is not allowed to operate where it has been specifically created with the intent to discriminate.

Other Legislation

Discrimination on the basis of pregnancy, childbirth, or related medical conditions is considered to be a form of sex discrimination, and is prohibited by the Pregnancy Discrimination Act of 1978. The law states that "women affected by pregnancy, childbirth, or related medical conditions shall be treated the same for all employment-related purposes . . . as other persons not so affected but similar in their ability or inability to work . . ."

A considerable portion of the differences in pay received by men and women is rooted in the concentration of women in a limited number of jobs that don't pay much, such as clerk and waitress. This lowers the overall average of the compensation received by women as compared to the overall average compensation received by men.

Is the low pay received by women in female-dominated jobs legal? The Equal Pay Act of 1963 prohibits companies from paying women less than men for the "same work." "Same work" under EPA is narrowly defined, however. To constitute the same work jobs must require equal skill, effort, and responsibility; be carried on under similar working conditions in the same location; and the work done must be the *same* or substantially similar, though not necessarily identical.

It is not easy for an organization woman in a managerial or professional position to prove that her job is the same in the legal sense as, for example, that of higher-paid male peers. It is easier to prove a woman's job and a man's are the same in cases of repetitive clearly-defined clerical and blue-collar jobs.

Title VII is more effective than the EPA in attacking wage differentials for men and women, particularly where class suits are involved and statistical comparisons can be used. Differences in pay for the very same job, for the same job carried on under different names, are clearly illegal. Differences in pay for the "same work" are also illegal. What about differences in pay for different jobs of the same "comparative worth"? It is being increasingly argued that women and men holding different jobs, but jobs of equal comparative worth, are legally entitled to equal pay under Title VII. How does one determine the comparative net worth of a female-dominated job, such as that of secretary, and a male-dominated job, such as that of janitor—to determine what the secretary should be getting paid in relation to the pay of the janitor, both working for the same employer in the same location? One tool for doing so is the use of job-evaluation studies. These rate, commonly by a point system, the requirements of different jobs as to knowledge and skills, mental demands, the degree of responsibility and accountability and working conditions. In one case, a study for Washington State, the job of truck driver (male) and that of laundry worker (female) rated about equally on points, though actual pay was about 30 percent less for the laundry worker than for the truck driver. Under a comparative worth concept both should be paid the same. This assumes, of course, that the job evaluation procedure used was a valid one and fairly carried out.

The concept of equal pay for jobs of equal comparable worth poses considerable legal problems. Eventually it is likely to gain acceptance, but slowly. It probably will require years of litigation to define the precise legal meaning of comparable worth, and substantively to address the very real problems of how to measure comparability.

The EEOC and Sexual Harassment

What about sexual harassment and the law? The Equal Employment Opportunity Commission in 1980 issued the following regarding sexual harassment. Such harassment is considered to be illegal sex discrimination in employment, under Title VII.

"Harassment on the basis of sex is a violation of Sec. 703 of Title VII. Unwelcome sexual advances, requests for sexual favors, and other verbal or physical conduct of a sexual nature constitute sexual harassment when (1) submission to such conduct is made either explicitly or implicitly a term or condition of an individual's employment, (2) submission or rejection of such conduct by an individual is used as the basis for employment decisions affecting such individual, or (3) such conduct has the purpose or effect of unreasonably interfering with an individual's work performance or creating an intimidating, hostile, or offensive working environment. . . .

"With respect to conduct between fellow employees, an employer is responsible for acts of sexual harassment in the work place where the employer (or its agents or supervisory employees) knows or should have known of the conduct, unless it can show that it took immediate and appropriate corrective action."

Sexual harassment is widespread. So long as men and women work together in the work place, and particularly so long as men are in positions of authority over women, it is likely that *some* harassment in *some* work environments will occur.

Dealing with sexual harassment is not easy. Often where harassment is persistent its victims have felt it necessary as a practical matter to find another job. Yet it *is* illegal, and it *can* be dealt with by legal action—filing an employment discrimination complaint with the EEOC and filing a lawsuit. Women *are* winning damages for assault and for emotional distress. But legal action is often a last resort insofar as it obviously risks retaliatory action. (Although retaliatory action is unlawful, it may be difficult to prove). Retaliatory action may be in terms of work assignments and treatment on the job, "nonsexual" harassment, ostracism, and loss of any opportunity for promotion in the future; or in actual discharge for "incompatibility," "inefficiency," or whatever; and in unfavorable references given to prospective new employers. An employer may side with the harasser rather than the harassed, if the employer believes the continued employment of the harasser is more important than is the continued employment of the harassee.

On the other hand, a lawsuit for sexual harassment can be embarrassing to an employer. The image of the company involved is not enhanced. Customers, especially but not only women, can be influenced adversely by publicity concerning sexual harassment. A lawsuit for sexual harassment can even be disconcerting to some executives personally in their contacts within the community. It's a sensitive matter. The very threat of a lawsuit may lead to rectifying a particular situation, with the corrective action necessary to insure discontinuance of harassment; and, it would be hoped, (but not with certainty) without adversely affecting the future career of the harassee within the organization. Or if the harassed employee does not remain an employee, a company may be willing to settle privately with the harassee for damages rather than go into court.

Further Employee Protection

What about age discrimination? This particularly affects women who after raising a family wish to enter or reenter the business world, and do. Under the Age Discrimination and Employment Act discrimination in hiring, dismissals, promotions, training, pay, other terms and conditions of employment and union membership against persons forty to seventy years old is illegal. Apprenticeship age requirements are excluded. The Act covers employers of 20 or more, public employers, employment agencies, and labor unions. The EEOC is given enforcement jurisdiction.

An employer cannot refuse to count an older person's experience where applicable as a substitute for educational qualifications. Neither is discrimination within the forty to seventy age range, say in favor of those in their forties, against those in their sixties, legal. Forced retirement of employees under age seventy is prohibited unless for legitimate business reasons. Also, among other items, an employer may not fire an older, higher-paid employee in order to hire a younger, less highly-paid person.

The use of bona fide occupational qualifications where truly valid is a legitimate defense against charge of age discrimination. Thus, age qualifications have been upheld for firefighters, police, and airline pilots.

What about the organization woman and unfair dismissal?

Aside from situations governed by antidiscrimination law and union contracts, employees generally are not protected from arbitrary dismissal. It has been the traditional rule that companies can fire employees for any reason or no reason at all. However, courts in a number of states, and particularly Michigan and California, have begun to challenge this traditional concept. The challenge frequently has been exercised on behalf of higher-level employees fired for whistle-blowing (for violations of law and illegal actions) against their employers. Bills have been introduced in the Michigan and California legislatures to prohibit by specific statute "unjust" or "wrongful" dismissals.

Each year countless American employees are fired, many of them unjustly, and many of them women. There is some belief that an increasing sensitivity by the citizenry to employee rights will lead to widespread state and eventually federal adoption of state and federal legislation aimed at protecting workers against arbitrary dismissal.

The field of women's rights in employment is one of active litigation and a dynamic changing area of the law. It therefore may be especially important to seek a lawyer's advice on particular problems that arise.

Appendix
The Questionnaires

*T*wo confidential questionnaires were used. These were to be filled out anonymously. The author emphasized that no signature or identification was asked for. Accordingly, only a few of the respondents did identify themselves on the completed returns. One questionnaire was addressed to men and the other to women employed in U.S. business organizations. Copies of the two forms are included below. The following mailings were used.

1. A mailing to a national random sampling of 1072 of the approximately 19,000 top executives of the "*Fortune* 1300." The latter is a listing of the 1,000 largest manufacturing corporations in the U.S. plus the 300 largest nonmanufacturing corporations in the U.S., as defined by the magazine *Fortune*. A purchased listing was used. Returns were 18 percent of 1056 (1072 less 16 returned on account of wrong addresses) forms mailed.

2. A mailing to a national random sampling of 1110 of approximately 39,000 women executives in corporations rated as having a net worth of $500,000 or more (purchased list). Separately questionnaires were mailed to 84 managerial and professional

women employed by large business organizations in the San Francisco Bay Area. Thus a total of 1149 addresses (1194 less 45 returned on account of wrong addresses) were sent forms. Returns were 20 percent.

3. A mailing went out to a random sample of 75 of the members of the San Francisco Bay Area Section of the Society of Women Engineers. Returns were 39 percent.

4. A mailing of six questionnaires, three for male executives and three for career women earning at least $25,000 annually, was addressed to a national sampling of the financial officers, generally the chief financial officer in each case, of 226 major U.S. corporations; with a request to each officer that he distribute the questionnaires within his company. Returns were 18 percent of the 678 questionnaires for men, and 18 percent of the 678 questionnaires for women.

At the cut-off point in time a total of 306 men's questionnaires (of 310 ultimately received) and 363 women's questionnaires (of 373 ultimately received) were tabulated. Respondents generally answered all or almost all questions. A minority omitted commenting on the three open-ended questions included at the end of each survey form.

Respondents were promised summaries of the survey results if they wished them and in separately mailed requests (to protect anonymity) asked for them. A substantial number of the respondents did so.

The mail surveys were conducted in 1982. They have been supplemented by personal interviews conducted in 1982-1984 with management people, both women and men.

FOR WOMEN
CONFIDENTIAL SURVEY
THE ORGANIZATION CAREER WOMAN

1. I WOULD GUESS THAT IN MY COMPANY MOST CAREER WOMEN, COMPARED TO MEN IN SIMILAR JOBS AND AT SIMILAR RESPONSIBILITY LEVELS —

   A. WORK: ☐ HARDER THAN;   ☐ ABOUT THE SAME AS;   ☐ NOT AS HARD AS MOST MEN.

   B. PERFORM: ☐ BETTER THAN;   ☐ ABOUT THE SAME AS;   ☐ NOT AS WELL AS MOST MEN.

   C. ARE PAID: ☐ BETTER THAN;   ☐ ABOUT THE SAME AS;   ☐ NOT AS WELL AS MOST MEN.

2. MY FEELING ABOUT THE PRESENT LIKELIHOOD OF A WOMAN IN THE FIRM BEING PROMOTED, IN COMPETITION WITH A MAN, GIVEN EQUAL QUALIFICATIONS AND EXPERIENCE, TO OR WITHIN THE FOLLOWING BRACKETS —

   A. JOBS PAYING $20,000 – $24,999 ANNUALLY: ☐ GREATER;   ☐ ABOUT THE SAME;   ☐ LESS FOR WOMEN.

   B. JOBS PAYING $25,000 – $34,999 ANNUALLY: ☐ GREATER;   ☐ ABOUT THE SAME;   ☐ LESS FOR WOMEN.

   C. JOBS PAYING $35,000 OR MORE ANNUALLY: ☐ GREATER;   ☐ ABOUT THE SAME;   ☐ LESS FOR WOMEN.

3. SOME WOMEN HAVE RECEIVED PROMOTIONS WHICH OTHERWISE WOULD HAVE GONE TO MEN. TO WHAT DEGREE DO THE MEN RESENT THIS? MY GUESS: ☐ NOT AT ALL;   ☐ A LITTLE;   ☐ SOMEWHAT;   ☐ A LOT.

4. **A.** TO A SIGNIFICANT DEGREE, I AM LOOKED UPON BY MEN IN MY PEER GROUP AS (MAY BE MULTIPLE ANSWERS)

   ☐ AN EQUAL;   ☐ AN EQUAL, **BUT;**   ☐ SOMEONE WHO HAS TO BE TOLERATED;
   ☐ AN UNWANTED COMPETITOR;   ☐ AN INFERIOR;   ☐ UNDULY FAVORED BECAUSE I AM A WOMAN;
   ☐ SOMEONE TO BE RESPECTED FOR HER ABILITIES.

   B. I SOCIALIZE WITH MALE COLLEAGUES —

   ON-THE-JOB (LUNCH, ETC.):   ☐ NOT MUCH;   ☐ SOMEWHAT;   ☐ A LOT.
   OFF-THE-JOB: ☐ NOT MUCH;   ☐ SOMEWHAT;   ☐ A LOT.

C. IN THE OFFICE, AND/OR AT COMPANY AFFAIRS, MEETINGS OR CONVENTIONS, I JOIN THE MEN IN:

	INFREQUENTLY OR NEVER	SOMETIMES	FREQUENTLY
USE OF PROFANITY	☐	☐	☐
DRINKING	☐	☐	☐
TELLING DIRTY STORIES	☐	☐	☐

D. IN GROUP MEETINGS WITHIN THE COMPANY, AS COMPARED TO MEN, I TAKE CARE OF —

MINUTES: ☐ MORE OFTEN; ☐ ABOUT AS OFTEN; ☐ NOT AT ALL; ☐ NOT RELEVANT.
COFFEE: ☐ MORE OFTEN; ☐ ABOUT AS OFTEN; ☐ NOT AT ALL; ☐ NOT RELEVANT.

5.
A. I TRAVEL ON THE JOB: ☐ A LOT; ☐ OCCASIONALLY; ☐ LITTLE OR NONE.
B. I TRAVEL ON THE JOB: ☐ GENERALLY ALONE; ☐ MOSTLY WITH ☐ FEMALE ☐ MALE COLLEAGUES
C. BECAUSE I AM A WOMAN, TRAVEL PRESENTS DIFFICULTIES: ☐ A LOT; ☐ SOMEWHAT; ☐ LITTLE/NONE

6.
A. I ENTERTAIN MEN (SUCH AS AT LUNCH OR DINNER OR THEATER) AS PART OF THE JOB:
☐ A LOT; ☐ SOMEWHAT; ☐ LITTLE OR NONE.
B. AS A WOMAN THIS PRESENTS — SOCIAL DIFFICULTIES: ☐ A LOT; ☐ SOMEWHAT; ☐ LITTLE/NONE
— SEXUAL DIFFICULTIES: ☐ A LOT; ☐ SOMEWHAT; ☐ LITTLE/NONE

7. I HAVE ☐ ACCEPTED; ☐ DECLINED; ☐ NOT BEEN OFFERED;
PROMOTION(S) INVOLVING A MOVE TO ANOTHER CITY.

8. MY OPINION AS TO THE VALUE OF THE FOLLOWING TO CAREER WOMEN IN FURTHERING THEIR ADVANCEMENT:

	SOME ADVANTAGE	A LITTLE ADVANTAGE	NO ADVANTAGE	DIS-ADVANTAGE
A. GOOD LOOKS	☐	☐	☐	☐
B. BEING SLENDER	☐	☐	☐	☐
C. DRESSING: SEXY MOST OF THE TIME	☐	☐	☐	☐
SEXY OCCASIONALLY	☐	☐	☐	☐
CONSERVATIVELY MOST OF THE TIME	☐	☐	☐	☐
CASUALLY MOST OF THE TIME	☐	☐	☐	☐
D. FLIRTING OCCASIONALLY	☐	☐	☐	☐
E. AN AFFAIR WITH THE BOSS OR OTHER INFLUENTIAL MALES	☐	☐	☐	☐

9. MY GUESS AS TO THE FREQUENCY WITH WHICH THE FOLLOWING OCCURS IN MY FIRM:

	NEVER OR RARELY	INFREQUENTLY BUT OCCASIONALLY	OFTEN
A. FLIRTING BY CAREER WOMEN	☐	☐	☐
B. AFFAIRS WITH THE BOSS OR OTHER INFLUENTIAL MALES	☐	☐	☐
C. AFFAIRS WITH NON-INFLUENTIAL MALES IN THE COMPANY	☐	☐	☐
D. SEXUAL HARASSMENT OF CAREER WOMEN:			
(1) ACTUAL INTIMACY	☐	☐	☐
(2) PROPOSED (AT LEAST SEMI-SERIOUSLY) INTIMACY	☐	☐	☐
(3) TOUCHING	☐	☐	☐
(4) VERBALLY OTHER THAN (2)	☐	☐	☐

E. USE OF SEXUAL CONNOTATION OR SEX ON THE JOB BY CAREER WOMEN:

	NEVER OR RARELY	INFREQUENTLY BUT OCCASIONALLY	OFTEN
(1) BY THE WAY THEY DRESS	☐	☐	☐
(2) BY APPEALS TO MALE GALLANTRY/PROTECTIVENESS	☐	☐	☐
(3) BY PROPOSING INTIMACY (AT LEAST SEMI-SERIOUSLY)	☐	☐	☐
(4) BY ACTUAL INTIMACY (WOMEN SEEK/ENCOURAGE)	☐	☐	☐
(5) BY VERBAL INNUENDO OR REPARTEE OTHER THAN (3)	☐	☐	☐

10. MY GUESS RE FEELINGS OF MEN'S WIVES TOWARDS CAREER WOMEN WHO WORK AS PEERS WITH THEIR HUSBANDS:

	LITTLE OR NONE	SOMEWHAT	A LOT
A. AFTER-HOURS OR OUT-OF-TOWN MEETINGS WHICH INCLUDE BOTH HUSBANDS AND CAREER WOMEN ARE RESENTED	☐	☐	☐
B. CAREER WOMEN ARE RESENTED IN GENERAL	☐	☐	☐

11. A. THE FIRST FULL TIME JOB I EVER HAD WAS AS AN _____.

   B. MY STARTING JOB WITH MY PRESENT EMPLOYER WAS AS _____ IN _____ (DEPARTMENT).

   C. I OBTAINED THIS STARTING JOB THROUGH:

   ☐ MY MAIL/TELEPHONE/PERSONAL INQUIRY;   ☐ ANSWERING AD;   ☐ MY AD(S);
   ☐ PROFESSIONAL RECRUITER/EMPLOYMENT AGENCY;   ☐ REFERRAL BY ☐ WOMAN, ☐ MAN I KNEW WHO:
   ☐ HAD BEEN WITH FORMER EMPLOYER OF MINE, ☐ WAS OR IS EMPLOYED BY MY PRESENT EMPLOYER,
   ☐ NEITHER;   ☐ REFERRAL THROUGH TRADE OR PROFESSIONAL ORGANIZATION;   ☐ OTHER _____

12. A. I HAVE BEEN WITH MY PRESENT EMPLOYER FOR ABOUT _____ YEARS.

   B. NUMBER OF MY **PRIOR** EMPLOYERS: ☐ NONE;   ☐ 1 OR 2;   ☐ 3 OR MORE.

13. **A.** REASONS FOR PROMOTION TO OR BEING HIRED INTO MY PRESENT JOB, IN ADDITION TO MY ABILITY AND PERFORM-
ANCE, INCLUDED TO A SIGNIFICANT DEGREE THE FOLLOWING (MAY BE MULTIPLE REASONS):
☐ "AFFIRMATIVE ACTION" EXPEDITED OPPORTUNITIES;   ☐ I REPLACED MY BOSS WHO GOT A NEW JOB;
☐ I REPLACED MY BOSS WHO RETIRED/RESIGNED/WAS FIRED;   ☐ I CREATED THE JOB;
☐ I WAS RECOMMENDED FOR THE JOB BY ☐ MY BOSS, ☐ SOMEONE ELSE; ☐ OTHER

B. THE INDIVIDUAL WHO ACTUALLY GAVE ME THE PROMOTION WAS A: ☐ MAN;   ☐ WOMAN.

C. THE PERSON TO WHOM I REPORT (MY IMMEDIATE BOSS) IS A   ☐ MAN;   ☐ WOMAN.

14. **A.** HAVE I EVER HAD A WOMAN SUPERVISOR?   ☐ YES;   ☐ NO.

B. IF I HAD A CHOICE, I WOULD LIKELY PREFER A   ☐ MALE;   ☐ FEMALE BOSS.

C. I WOULD GUESS THAT MOSTLY, A   ☐ MALE,   ☐ FEMALE BOSS   IS THE MORE DEMANDING.

15. HAS THERE BEEN ANY ONE INDIVIDUAL   ☐ IN THE COMPANY I NOW WORK FOR, OR   ☐ WHOM I'VE WORKED FOR IN THE
PAST, WHO HAS BEEN OUTSTANDINGLY HELPFUL TO ME IN MY CAREER?   ☐ YES;   ☐ NO.
IF YES, THAT INDIVIDUAL WAS A   ☐ MAN;   ☐ WOMAN; AND ☐ MY IMMEDIATE BOSS;   ☐ HIS BOSS;   ☐ OTHER.

16. **A.** IS INCREASE IN JOB STRESS WITH CAREER ADVANCEMENT LIKELY TO DETER ME IN THE FUTURE FROM SEEKING AD-
DITIONAL PROMOTIONS?   ☐ YES;   ☐ NO;   ☐ NO INCREASE IN STRESS.

B. I USE THE FOLLOWING TO COPE WITH JOB STRESS:
☐ JOGGING;   ☐ SPAS OR EXERCISE GYMS/CLUBS;   ☐ ACTIVE SPORTS;   ☐ FOOD/SWEETS BINGES;
☐ CIGARETTES;   ☐ ALCOHOL;   ☐ TRANQUILIZERS/OTHER DRUGS;   ☐ OTHER

17. I PLAN TO CONTINUE WITH A FULL-TIME CAREER IN EITHER MY PRESENT OR ANOTHER ORGANIZATION UNTIL AT LEAST
THE AGE OF 60:
☐ YES, CONTINUALLY;   ☐ YES, WITH TIME OFF FOR   ☐ CHILDREN,   ☐ OTHER;   ☐ NO;   ☐ DON'T KNOW.

18. MY GUESS RE WHETHER THE FOLLOWING LIKELY WOULD CREATE A SIGNIFICANT PROBLEM FOR MOST CAREER WOMEN:

	YES	NO
A. EARNINGS OF WOMAN EXCEEDING HUSBAND'S	☐	☐
B. HUSBAND'S WORKING FOR THE SAME EMPLOYER AS WIFE	☐	☐
C. WOMAN OFTEN TRAVELING OUT-OF-TOWN:		
2 OR 3 DAYS AT A TIME	☐ ☐ ☐	☐ ☐ ☐
LONGER THAN 3 DAYS AT A TIME		
D. WOMAN BRINGING AT-WORK PROBLEMS INTO THE HOME	☐	☐

19. PLEASE ANSWER THIS ONLY IF YOU ARE NOW MARRIED:

	YES	NO
A. MY EARNINGS EXCEED THOSE OF MY HUSBAND'S:	☐	☐
B. MY HUSBAND AND I WORK FOR THE SAME EMPLOYER:	☐	☐

C. IF NECESSARY TO MOVE TO ANOTHER CITY TO ADVANCE MY CAREER, I EXPECT TO ☐ DO SO; ☐ NOT TO DO SO
BECAUSE OF MY HUSBAND'S CAREER; ☐ NOT TO DO SO FOR OTHER REASONS.

D. THE HOUSEHOLD CHORES ARE MOSTLY: ☐ MINE; ☐ MY HUSBAND'S; ☐ BOTH; ☐ NEITHER.

20. PLEASE ANSWER THIS ONLY IF YOU ARE NOW OR HAVE BEEN MARRIED.

	HURT		HELPED		DON'T
	A BIT	SOMEWHAT	A BIT	SOMEWHAT	NEITHER KNOW
CAREER'S EFFECT ON MY MARRIAGE	☐	☐	☐	☐	☐ ☐
MARRIAGE'S EFFECT ON MY CAREER	☐	☐	☐	☐	☐ ☐
CAREER'S EFFECT ON QUALITY OF MY LIFE	☐	☐	☐	☐	☐ ☐
COMBINATION'S EFFECT ON MY HEALTH	☐	☐	☐	☐	☐ ☐

21. A. IF FINANCIAL CONSIDERATIONS AFTER MARRIAGE WERE UNIMPORTANT IN THE PAST, WOULD I HAVE HAD A CAREER AFTER MARRIAGE (FOR THOSE NOW MARRIED)? ☐ YES; ☐ NO; ☐ NOT SURE.

B. ARE FINANCIAL CONSIDERATIONS NOW UNIMPORTANT RE MY CAREER? ☐ YES; ☐ NO.

C. IF FINANCIAL CONSIDERATIONS WERE NOW UNIMPORTANT, WOULD I KEEP ON WITH MY CAREER NOW?
☐ YES; ☐ NO; ☐ NOT SURE.

22. WHAT I CONSIDER TO BE THE MOST IMPORTANT FACTOR(S), IN ADDITION TO JOB PERFORMANCE, FOR A WOMAN'S GETTING AHEAD IN MY COMPANY: _____

_____

_____

23. WHAT I CONSIDER TO BE THE GREATEST OBSTACLE(S) TO A WOMAN'S GETTING AHEAD IN MY COMPANY: _____

_____

24. WHAT I CONSIDER TO BE THE MOST DIFFICULT, IRRITATING, FRUSTRATING AND/OR DISTASTEFUL PROBLEM(S) FOR ME AS A WOMAN WORKING WITH —

A. MEN: _____

_____

_____

B. OTHER WOMEN: _____

_____

_____

25. **A.** SIZE OF MY COMPANY — TOTAL NUMBER OF EMPLOYEES (AT ALL LOCATIONS):
□ UNDER 500; □ 500 – 999; □ 1,000 OR MORE.

B. MY AGE: □ UNDER 30; □ 30 – 39; □ 40 – 49; □ 50 AND OVER.

C. MY PRESENT SALARY (INCLUSIVE OF EXPECTED BONUS/COMMISSIONS THIS YEAR):
□ LESS THAN $25,000; □ $25,000 – 29,999; □ $30,000 – 34,999; □ $35,000 AND OVER.

D. □ MARRIED; □ SINGLE; □ SEPARATED OR DIVORCED; □ WIDOWED; □ LIVING WITH MAN.

E. I HAVE CHILDREN UNDER 18: □ YES; □ NO.

F. MY TITLE (AND DEPARTMENT): _____

G. NUMBER OF PERSONS REPORTING TO ME DIRECTLY OR THROUGH SUBORDINATES, IS ABOUT _____.
THESE ARE: □ 0 – 29% MEN; □ 30 – 69% MEN; □ 70 – 100% MEN.

H. I PREFER TO BE ADDRESSED AS: □ MRS.; □ MISS; □ MS.

26. ON A SEPARATE SHEET OF PAPER PLEASE NOTE ANY COMMENTS YOU CARE TO ADD TO THE ABOVE; OR ON CAREER WOMEN'S PERSONAL VS. JOB PRIORITIES; ON CHILDREN; ON CHILD CARE FACILITIES; ETC.

IT IS NOT NECESSARY TO SIGN YOUR NAME OR GIVE THE NAME OF YOUR ORGANIZATION.

CONFIDENTIAL

FOR MEN
CONFIDENTIAL SURVEY
THE ORGANIZATION CAREER WOMAN

1. I WOULD GUESS THAT IN MY COMPANY, FOR MOST WOMEN EARNING $25,000 OR MORE ANNUALLY, COMPARED TO MOST MEN IN SIMILAR JOBS AND AT SIMILAR RESPONSIBILITY LEVELS —

A. CHARACTERISTICS — WOMEN COMPARED TO MEN:

	WOMEN TEND TO BE		
	MORE	ABOUT SAME	LESS
HARD WORKING	☐	☐	☐
EFFECTIVE IN JOB PERFORMANCE	☐	☐	☐
INTELLIGENT	☐	☐	☐
SKILLED AND KNOWLEDGEABLE IN JOB	☐	☐	☐
PRACTICAL	☐	☐	☐
QUALITY-MINDED IN WORK/PRODUCT OUTPUT	☐	☐	☐
INNOVATIVE/CREATIVE	☐	☐	☐
WELL ORGANIZED IN THEIR WORK	☐	☐	☐
ABLE TO COPE WITH CRISES	☐	☐	☐
HONEST (NO "SHADING," COVER-UP, DISTORTION)	☐	☐	☐
ABSENT FROM WORK — ILLNESS, ETC.	☐	☐	☐
LIKELY TO REMAIN WITH ORGANIZATION FOR MANY YEARS	☐	☐	☐
EMOTIONAL	☐	☐	☐
DECISIVE	☐	☐	☐
RUTHLESS	☐	☐	☐
CONSIDERATE	☐	☐	☐
DEVIOUS	☐	☐	☐
OBSTINATE	☐	☐	☐
DIPLOMATIC	☐	☐	☐
VINDICTIVE	☐	☐	☐
AGGRESSIVE	☐	☐	☐
DEMANDING OF SUBORDINATE MEN	☐	☐	☐

DEMANDING OF SUBORDINATE WOMEN ☐☐☐☐☐☐ ☐☐☐☐☐☐ ☐☐☐☐☐☐
ARTICULATE
SENSITIVE TO CRITICISM
SENSITIVE TO ORGANIZATIONAL INTERRELATIONSHIPS
ABLE TO MOTIVATE MALE SUBORDINATES
ABLE TO MOTIVATE FEMALE SUBORDINATES

B. WILLING TO: ☐☐☐☐ ☐☐☐☐ ☐☐☐☐
TAKE CALCULATED RISKS
DELEGATE
BACK UP A SUBORDINATE
TAKE ON NEW RESPONSIBILITY

**C. IN RELATIONSHIPS WITH SUBORDINATES, WILLING TO DO THE
FOLLOWING — WOMEN COMPARED TO MEN:** ☐☐☐☐☐☐ ☐☐☐☐☐☐ ☐☐☐☐☐☐
SEEK ADVICE/OPINIONS FROM SUBORDINATES
TAKE, AND NOT GIVE CREDIT FOR IDEAS/WORK
FAVOR MEN AS A GROUP OVER WOMEN
FAVOR WOMEN AS A GROUP OVER MEN
PLAY FAVORITES WITH PARTICULAR INDIVIDUALS
BE FAIR

2. I WOULD GUESS THAT AS TO CAREER WOMEN IN MY COMPANY EARNING $25,000 OR MORE ANNUALLY —
   A. MOST ARE: ☐ NOW MARRIED; ☐ NOT NOW MARRIED.
   B. MOST HOLD: ☐ LINE; ☐ STAFF POSITIONS.
   C. THOSE IN LINE POSITIONS MOSTLY SUPERVISE GROUPS MADE UP OF: ☐ 70–100% MEN;
   ☐ 30–69% MEN; ☐ 0–29% MEN.
   D. THE PROPORTION OF ALL, LINE AND STAFF, WHO WILL CONTINUE WITH A FULL TIME CAREER UNTIL AT LEAST THE AGE OF 60:
   ☐ 80% OR MORE; ☐ 60–80%; ☐ ABOUT HALF; ☐ 30–40%; ☐ LESS THAN 30%.

3. MY GUESS AS TO WHERE IN THE COMPANY ONE FINDS THE GREATEST NUMBER OF WOMEN EARNING ANNUALLY:

	$25,000 - 34,999			$35,000 & OVER		
	MOST	2ND MOST	3RD MOST	MOST	2ND MOST	3RD MOST
GENERAL OR OFFICE ADMINISTRATION	☐	☐	☐	☐	☐	☐
OPERATIONS (PRODUCING PRODUCTS/SERVICES SOLD)	☐	☐	☐	☐	☐	☐
MARKETING/SALES/MARKET RESEARCH	☐	☐	☐	☐	☐	☐
ADVERTISING/PROMOTION/PUBLIC RELATIONS	☐	☐	☐	☐	☐	☐
ELECTRONIC DATA PROCESSING (EDP)	☐	☐	☐	☐	☐	☐
ACCOUNTING/FINANCE (NOT EDP)	☐	☐	☐	☐	☐	☐
PERSONNEL	☐	☐	☐	☐	☐	☐
ENGINEERING/R&D (TECHNICAL)	☐	☐	☐	☐	☐	☐
OTHER _____	☐	☐	☐	☐	☐	☐

4. MY GUESS AS TO MY COMPANY'S CURRENT SOURCES FOR RECRUITING WOMEN FOR JOBS PAYING ANNUALLY:

	$25,000 - 34,999			$35,000 & OVER		
	MOST OFTEN	2ND MOST	3RD MOST	MOST OFTEN	2ND MOST	3RD MOST
INTERNAL PROMOTION	☐	☐	☐	☐	☐	☐
PROFESSIONAL RECRUITERS/EMPLOYMENT AGENCIES	☐	☐	☐	☐	☐	☐
REFERRALS FROM EMPLOYEES/ASSOCIATES/OTHERS	☐	☐	☐	☐	☐	☐
CO.'S PAID ADVERTISING OF JOB OPENINGS	☐	☐	☐	☐	☐	☐
APPLICANT ADS OR INQUIRIES	☐	☐	☐	☐	☐	☐
OTHER _____	☐	☐	☐	☐	☐	☐

5. MY FEELING ABOUT THE PRESENT LIKELIHOOD OF A WOMAN IN THE FIRM BEING PROMOTED, IN COMPETITION WITH A MAN, GIVEN EQUAL QUALIFICATIONS AND EXPERIENCE, TO OR WITHIN THE FOLLOWING BRACKETS —

JOBS PAYING $25,000 – 34,999 ANNUALLY: ☐ GREATER; ☐ ABOUT THE SAME; ☐ LESS FOR WOMEN.
JOBS PAYING $35,000 OR MORE ANNUALLY: ☐ GREATER; ☐ ABOUT THE SAME; ☐ LESS FOR WOMEN.

6. SOME WOMEN HAVE RECEIVED PROMOTIONS WHICH OTHERWISE WOULD HAVE GONE TO MEN. TO WHAT DEGREE DO MEN RESENT THIS? MY GUESS: ☐ NOT AT ALL; ☐ A LITTLE; ☐ SOMEWHAT; ☐ A LOT.

7. IT IS MY FEELING THAT A WOMAN IN THE COMPANY WHO EARNS $25,000 OR MORE ANNUALLY IS OFTEN LIKELY TO BE LOOKED UPON BY THE MEN IN HER PEER GROUP AS (MAY BE MULTIPLE ANSWERS):
☐ AN EQUAL;   ☐ AN EQUAL, **BUT**;   ☐ SOMEONE WHO HAS TO BE TOLERATED;
☐ AN UNWANTED COMPETITOR;   ☐ SOMEONE UNDULY FAVORED BECAUSE SHE IS A WOMAN;
☐ SOMEONE TO BE RESPECTED FOR HER ABILITIES.

8. MY GUESS RE FEELINGS OF MEN'S WIVES TOWARDS CAREER WOMEN WHO WORK AS PEERS WITH THEIR HUSBANDS:

	LITTLE OR NONE	SOMEWHAT	A LOT
A. AFTER-HOURS OR OUT-OF-TOWN MEETINGS WHICH INCLUDE BOTH HUSBANDS AND CAREER WOMEN ARE RESENTED	☐	☐	☐
B. CAREER WOMEN ARE RESENTED IN GENERAL	☐	☐	☐

9. MY OPINION AS TO THE VALUE OF THE FOLLOWING TO CAREER WOMEN IN FURTHERING THEIR ADVANCEMENT:

	SOME ADVANTAGE	A LITTLE ADVANTAGE	NO ADVANTAGE	DIS-ADVANTAGE
A. GOOD LOOKS	☐	☐	☐	☐
B. BEING SLENDER	☐	☐	☐	☐
C. DRESSING: SEXY MOST OF THE TIME	☐	☐	☐	☐
SEXY OCCASIONALLY	☐	☐	☐	☐
CONSERVATIVELY MOST OF THE TIME	☐	☐	☐	☐
CASUALLY MOST OF THE TIME	☐	☐	☐	☐
D. SOCIALIZING WITH MALE COLLEAGUES ON-THE-JOB (LUNCH, ETC.)	☐	☐	☐	☐
OFF-THE-JOB	☐	☐	☐	☐
E. JOINING WITH MEN IN THE USE OF PROFANITY	☐	☐	☐	☐
F. FLIRTING OCCASIONALLY	☐	☐	☐	☐
G. AN AFFAIR WITH THE BOSS/OTHER INFLUENTIAL MALES	☐	☐	☐	☐

10. MY GUESS AS TO THE FREQUENCY WITH WHICH THE FOLLOWING OCCURS IN MY FIRM:

	NEVER OR RARELY	INFREQUENTLY BUT OCCASIONALLY	OFTEN
A. FLIRTING BY CAREER WOMEN	☐	☐	☐
B. AFFAIRS WITH THE BOSS OR OTHER INFLUENTIAL MALES	☐	☐	☐
C. AFFAIRS WITH NON-INFLUENTIAL MALES IN THE COMPANY			
D. SEXUAL HARASSMENT OF CAREER WOMEN:			
(1) ACTUAL INTIMACY	☐	☐	☐
(2) PROPOSED (AT LEAST SEMI-SERIOUSLY) INTIMACY	☐	☐	☐
(3) TOUCHING	☐	☐	☐
(4) VERBALLY OTHER THAN (2)	☐	☐	☐

E. USE OF SEXUAL CONNOTATION OR SEX ON THE JOB BY CAREER WOMEN:

	NEVER OR RARELY	INFREQUENTLY BUT OCCASIONALLY	OFTEN
(1) BY THE WAY THEY DRESS	☐	☐	☐
(2) BY APPEALS TO MALE GALLANTRY/PROTECTIVENESS	☐	☐	☐
(3) BY PROPOSING INTIMACY (AT LEAST SEMI-SERIOUSLY)	☐	☐	☐
(4) BY ACTUAL INTIMACY (WOMEN SEEK/ENCOURAGE)	☐	☐	☐
(5) BY VERBAL INNUENDO OR REPARTEE OTHER THAN (3)	☐	☐	☐

11. MY OPINION AS TO WHETHER MARRIAGE IS LIKELY TO INTERFERE WITH, OR TO IMPROVE THE ABILITY OF A CAREER WOMAN TO —

	INTERFERE WITH	IMPROVE	NEITHER
A. WITHOUT CHILDREN:			
DO HER JOB WELL	☐	☐	☐
ADVANCE IN HER CAREER	☐	☐	☐
B. WITH CHILDREN:			
DO HER JOB WELL	☐	☐	☐
ADVANCE IN HER CAREER	☐	☐	☐

APPENDIX • 165

12. WHAT I CONSIDER TO BE THE MOST IMPORTANT FACTOR(S), IN ADDITION TO JOB PERFORMANCE, FOR A WOMAN'S GETTING AHEAD IN MY COMPANY: _____

13. WHAT I CONSIDER TO BE THE GREATEST OBSTACLE(S) TO A WOMAN'S GETTING AHEAD IN MY COMPANY: _____

14. WHAT I CONSIDER TO BE THE MOST DIFFICULT, IRRITATING, FRUSTRATING AND/OR DISTASTEFUL PROBLEM(S) IN WORKING WITH CAREER WOMEN: _____

15. A. SIZE OF MY COMPANY — TOTAL NUMBER OF EMPLOYEES (AT ALL LOCATIONS):
    ☐ UNDER 500;   ☐ 500 – 999;   ☐ 1,000 OR MORE.
    B. MY AGE: ☐ UNDER 30;   ☐ 30 – 39;   ☐ 40 – 49;   ☐ 50 AND OVER.
    C. MY TITLE _____
    D. NUMBER OF PERSONS REPORTING TO ME DIRECTLY OR THROUGH MY SUBORDINATES IS ABOUT _____ .

ON A SEPARATE SHEET OF PAPER PLEASE NOTE ANY COMMENTS YOU CARE TO MAKE ABOUT OR ADD TO ANY OF THE POINTS COVERED ABOVE; OR OTHERWISE ABOUT OR TO WOMEN SEEKING A CAREER, OR ADVANCEMENT THEREIN; OR ON THE FUTURE FOR WOMEN SEEKING A CAREER.

IT IS NOT NECESSARY TO SIGN YOUR NAME OR GIVE THE NAME OF YOUR ORGANIZATION.

CONFIDENTIAL

Tables

Table 1

Profile of Survey Respondents
Figures Are in Percent

	Women	Men
Size of employing company:		
Under 500 employees	34	1
500–999 employees	8	5
1,000 or more employees	58	94
	100	100
Age:		
Under 30	12	2
30–39	41	19
40–49	25	36
50 and over	22	43
	100	100
Salary (1982)—asked of women only:		
Less than $25,000	19	
$25,000–29,999	18	
$30,000–34,999	16	
$35,000 and over	47	
	100	
Marital status—asked of women only:		
Married	55	
Single	20	
Separated or divorced	20	
Widowed	2	
Living with man	3	
	100	

Children under 18—asked of women only
(figures are for those married, plus separated
or divorced, plus widowed):

Yes	33	
No	67	
	100	

Position held:

President or Chief Executive Officer	*3	**4
Executive vice president	1.2	8.5
Senior vice president	1.2	12.7
Vice president	24.2	36.9
Company director	0.6	1.2
Subtotal	27	59
Secretary and/or Treasurer	5	1
Corporate Secretary	4	0
Managers or directors of functions, activities or operations—women mostly staff; men—mixed, both line and staff	33	27
Assistants or "assistants to" for above	3	4
Office managers	3	0
Engineers/allied professionals	7	0
Attorneys	2	1
Specialists (purchasing agents, analysts, etc.)	11	4
Secretarial (not corporate secretary or "assistant to" corporate secretary)	2	0
TOTAL	100	100

Number of persons reporting to the respondent,
directly or through subordinates:

None	24	
1–3	21	
4–5	16	
6–10	9	
11–20	10	
Over 20	20	
0–20		36
21–50		13
51–100		16
Over 100		35
TOTAL	100	100

*Includes 2 owners of small companies, 6 presidents and 2 newspaper editors
**Includes 9 presidents and 2 CEOs.

Table 2

Male Respondents' Perceptions of Organization (Better-Paid Career) Women

General Characteristics

Figures Are in Percent

"I would guess that in my company, for most women earning $25,000 or more annually (1982 dollars), compared to most men in similar jobs and at similar responsibility levels . . ."

Grouped according to related or somewhat related characteristics, to facilitate reader comparisons.

| | Women Tend to be | | |
	More	Less	About Same
1. **Group 1**			
More than men			
Hard working	29	2	69
Intelligent	21	2	77
Well organized in their work	36	7	57
Willing to take on new responsibilities	22	8	70
Quality-minded in work/product output	34	2	64
About same as men			
Innovative/creative	19	11	70
Skilled and knowledgeable in job	11	13	76
Less than men			
Practical	7	28	65
About same as men			
Effective in job performance	8	9	83
2. **Group 2**			
More than men			
Emotional	49	5	46
Sensitivity to criticism	22	12	66
Less than men			
Ability to cope with crises	4	37	59
3. **Group 3**			
About same as men			
Aggressive	21	21	58
Obstinate	13	15	72

Less than men

Decisive	5	21	74
Willing to take calculated risks	4	37	59

4. **Group 4**

More than men

Articulate	25	2	73
Diplomatic	27	8	65
Sensitive to organizational interrelationships	22	12	56

5. **Group 5**

Honest (No "shading," cover-up, distortion)	25	4	71
Devious	8	22	70

6. **Group 6**

More than men

Considerate	29	5	66

Less than men

Ruthless	8	35	57
Vindictive	11	17	72

7. **Group 7**

Absent from work—illness, etc.	22	9	69

Table 3

Male Respondents' Perceptions of Organization Women

Relationships with Subordinates

Figures Are in Percent

"I would guess that in my company, for most women earning $25,000 or more annually (1982 dollars), compared to most men in similar jobs and at similar responsibility levels . . ."

	Women Tend to be		
	More	**Less**	**About Same**
1. **More Demanding**			
Of subordinate men	8	9	83
Of subordinate women	34	2	64

Opinions of women surveyed (to compare with men):

"I guess that mostly a . . ."

Male boss is the more demanding	30
Female boss is the more demanding	55
Depends on the individual	15
	100

"If I had a choice I would likely prefer a . . ."

Male boss	62
Female boss	18
Depends on the individual	20
	100

	More	Less	About Same
2. Favor men as a group over women	18	10	72
Favor women as a group over men	11	18	71
Play favorites with particular individuals	15	7	78
3. Willing to:			
Seek advice/opinions from subordinates	20	18	62
Give and not take credit for ideas/work	14	9	77
Back up a subordinate	11	7	82
Be fair	10	6	84
4. Willing to delegate	6	25	77
5. Ability to motivate			
Male subordinates	2	21	77
Female subordinates	9	18	73

Table 4

Permanence of a Woman's Employment

Figures Are in Percent

| | Women Tend to be | | |
	More	Less	About Same
1. Male respondents' perceptions—Likely to remain with organization for many years	17	38	45

2. Additionally male respondents have expressed the opinion that the "proportion of all women in my company who earn $25,000 or more annually who will continue with a full-time career until at least the age of 60, is . . ."

Less than 30%	12
30 to 40%	12
About half	31
60% to 80%	24
80% or more	21
	100

3. The women surveyed claim they "plan to continue with a full-time career in either my present or another organization until at least the age of 60:"

Yes, continually		69
Yes, with time off		20
For children	12	
Other	8	
No		2
Don't know		9
		100

4. The women surveyed additionally have indicated that "If financial considerations were now unimportant, would I keep on with my career now?"

Yes	77
No	6
Not Sure	17
	100

Financial considerations are claimed to be indeed important by 74% of the women surveyed.

For those now married, 75% of the women surveyed claim they would have had a career after marriage even if financial considerations had not been important; 7% claim they would not have had a career; and 17% are not sure whether they would have had one or not.

Table 5

The Jobs Held by the Organization Women Surveyed

Figures Are in Percent

1. The jobs held by the women surveyed are chiefly staff (advisory) rather than line (command).

    A. Their job titles and departments so indicate.

    B. The numbers of persons reporting to them, either directly or through subordinates, as reported by the women surveyed, so indicate. See Table 1.

    C. The men surveyed so indicate in answer to "I would guess as to career women in my company earning $25,000 or more annually . . ."

Most hold staff positions	76
Most hold line positions	24
	100

2. Those supervised by the organization women are mostly women.

    A. Women surveyed: The "persons reporting to me directly or through subordinates are . . ."

0 – 29% men	65
30 – 69% men	23
70 – 100% men	12
	100

    B. Men surveyed: Women "in line positions mostly supervise groups made up of . . ."

0 – 29% men	45
30 – 69% men	41
70 – 100% men	14
	100

3. A woman's progress is predominantly determined by men.

    A. Women surveyed: "The person to whom I report (my immediate boss) is a . . ."

Man	95
Woman	5
	100

    B. Women surveyed: "Have I ever had a woman supervisor?"

Yes (in earlier jobs, generally)	54
No	46
	100

C. Women surveyed: "The individual who actually gave me the promotion]to my present job] was a . . ."

Man	96
Woman	4
	100

D. Women surveyed: "Has there been any one individual in the company I now work for, or whom I've worked for in the past, who has been outstandingly helpful in my career?"

Man	86	(of the 81% responding who answered "Yes")
Woman	14	
	100	

Table 6

Where in the Company the Better-Paid Jobs for Women are Found

Figures Are in Percent

"My guess as to where in the company one finds the greatest number of women earning annually . . ."]Responses are those of the men surveyed]:

	$25,000–34,999			$35,000 & Over		
	Most	2nd Most	3rd Most	Most	2nd Most	3rd Most
General or Office Admin.	25	13	11	33	11	14
Operations (Producing Products/ Services Sold)	5	7	13	4	7	14
Marketing/Sales/Market Research	15	17	12	18	17	12
Advertising/Promotion/ Public Relations	6	14	11	9	14	10
Electronic Data Processing (EDP)	14	14	11	7	13	10
Accounting/Finance (Not EDP)	14	15	16	8	18	15
Personnel	14	15	16	10	13	12
Engineering/R&D (Technical)	4	4	9	5	4	11
Other	3	1	1	6	3	2
	100	100	100	100	100	100

Table 7

How Jobs Are Obtained

1. A. "The first full-time job I ever had was . . ."
   B. "My starting job with my present employer was as . . ."

	A	B
Secretary	20	18
Typist, bookkeeper, clerk, and pink collar not classified otherwise	33	20
Sales/sales clerk/customer service	4	4
Technical or other job requiring specialized talent/skill/training/experience not classified otherwise	12	11
Professional	20	19
Supervisor/administrator or assistant, manager, or assistant, or supervisory/administrative/management trainee	7	27
Blue Collar	4	1
	100	100

Note:
1. The importance of the secretary classification for both A and B.
2. The importance of the pink collar classification, but less so for B than for A.
3. The low figure for sales/sales clerk/customer service.
4. The sharply higher "supervisory/managerial" figure for B as compared with A.
5. The low figure for the blue collar.

2. Women surveyed: "I obtained this starting job [with my present employer] through . . ."

My mail/telephone/personal inquiry	15
Answering ad	14
My ad(s)	0
Professional recruiter/employment agency	25

Referral by

Woman I knew	9)	26
Man I knew	17)	
Who had been with former employer of mine	5)	26
Was or is employed by my present employer	14)	
Neither	7)	

Referral through trade or professional organization	3
Other—school, etc.	17
	100

3. "My guess as to my company's current sources for recruiting women for jobs paying annually . . ." [Responses are those of the men surveyed]:

	$25,000–34,999			$35,000 & Over		
	Most	2nd Most	3rd Most	Most	2nd Most	3rd Most
Internal Promotion	68	15	8	62	19	12
Professional Recruiters/ Employment Agencies	17	36	20	27	38	15
Referrals from Employees/ Associates/Others	5	20	24	5	23	21
Company's Paid Advertising of Openings	3	15	28	3	13	23
Applicant Ads or Inquiries	3	11	19	2	7	17
Other	4	3	1	1	0	2
	100	100	100	100	100	100

Note: The most important source for recruiting appears to be internal promotion. For hiring from the outside, professional recruiters/employment agencies ranks first, followed by referrals which ranks second. Item 2, above, ranks referrals higher than professional recruiters/employment agencies. Item 2 refers to *starting* jobs with the present employer, however, and those jobs by no means all started with $25,000 and over.

In any case, both sources are important and both outrank company advertising or applicant ads/inquiries.

Table 8

Reasons for Promotion, Other Than Ability and Performance Figures Are in Percent

"Reasons for promotion to or being hired into my present job, in addition to my ability and performance, included to a significant degree the following (may be multiple reasons). [Responses are those of the women, in percent of those surveyed.]

"Affirmative action" expedited opportunities		21
I replaced my boss who got a new job		9
I replaced my boss who retired/resigned/was fired		12
I created the job		15
I was recommended for the job		63
By my boss	43	
By someone else	20	
Other		7

Note: The importance of "affirmative action" may be understated. There could be a reluctance in some cases to attribute promotion to this factor. It may be more self-reassuring to emphasize the importance of one's ability to replace the boss, being able to create a job, getting recommended. Affirmative action has undoubtedly often been the unacknowledged prod for getting a woman promoted, even though ability and performance have been requisites.

Table 9

Job Turnover
Figures Are in Percent

1. "I have been with my present employer for about . . ." [Responses are those of the women surveyed.]

0 – 3 years	22
4 – 5	15
6 – 10	21
11 – 20	29
Over 20	13
	100

Median — 9 years

2. "Number of my prior employers . . ." [Responses are those of the women surveyed.]

None	12
1 or 2	46
3 or more	42
	100

Table 10

Stress
Figures Are in Percent

1. Women surveyed: "Is increase in job stress with career advancement likely to deter me in the future from seeking additional promotions?"

Yes	20
No	74
No increase in stress	6
	100

2. Women surveyed: "I use the following to cope with stress"—multiple responses—In percent of 363 tabulated returns:

Jogging	12
Spas or exercise gyms/clubs	25
Active sports	25
Food/sweets binges	14
Cigarettes	27
Alcohol	19
Tranquilizers/other drugs	3
Other—home, social activities, etc.	34

Table 11

Job Problems Faced by Women
Figures Are in Percent

1. **Travel** [data are from the responses of the women surveyed.]

    A. "I travel on the job . . ."

A lot	19
Occasionally	47
Little/none	34
	100

    B. "I travel on the job . . ."

Generally alone		61
Mostly with colleagues		39
Male	33	
Female	6	
		100

    C. "Because I am a woman, travel presents difficulties . . ."

A lot	4
Somewhat	20
Little/none	76
	100

    D. "My guess re: whether the following likely would create a significant problem for most career women . . ."

	Yes	No
Woman often traveling out-of-town		
2 or 3 days at a time	42	58
Longer than 3 days at a time	73	27

2. **Entertaining** [data are from responses of the women surveyed]:

    A. "I entertain men (such as at lunch or dinner or theater) as part of the job . . ."

A lot	13
Somewhat	33
Little or none	54
	100

(continued on next page)

(continued from previous page)

B. "As a woman this presents social difficulties . . ."

A lot	3
Somewhat	17
Little or none	80
	100

C. "As a woman this presents sexual difficulties . . ."

A lot	2
Somewhat	15
Little or none	83
	100

3. Socializing

A. "My opinion as to the value of the following to career women in furthering their advancement . . ." [data are from the responses of the men surveyed]:

Socializing with male colleagues	On-the-job (lunch, etc.)	Off-the job
Some advantage	26	8
A little advantage	38	20
No advantage	34	47
Disadvantage	2	25
	100	100

B. "I socialize with male colleagues . . ." [data are from the responses of the women surveyed]:

	On-the-job (lunch, etc.)	Off-the job
Not much	27	68
Somewhat	43	26
A lot	30	6
	100	100

C. "My opinion as to the value of the following to career women in furthering their advancement . . ." [data are from the responses of the men surveyed]:

Joining with men in the use of profanity

Some advantage	0.3
A little advantage	2
No advantage	35
Disadvantage	63
	100

D. "In the office, and/or at company affairs, meetings or conventions, I join the men in . . ." [data are from the responses of the women surveyed]:

	Infrequently or never	Some times	Frequently
Use of profanity	69	27	4
Drinking	28	50	22
Telling dirty stories	88	11	1

4. **Transfers** [data are from the responses of the women surveyed]:

A. "I have, re: promotion(s) involving a move to another city . . ."

Accepted	10	of *all* women
Declined	16	
Not been offered	74	
	100	

B. "If necessary to move to another city to advance my career, I expect to . . ." [data are from responses of married women only]:

Do so	31
Not do so because of my husband's career	20
Not do so for other reasons	49
	100

5. "My guess re: whether the following likely would create a significant problem for most [married] career women . . ." [data are from the responses of all the women, married plus unmarried, surveyed]:

Woman bringing at-work problems into the home:

Yes	66
No	34
	100

6. "In group meetings within the company, as compared to men, I take care of . . ." [data are from the responses of the women surveyed]:

	Minutes	Coffee
More often	20	12
About as often	14	42
Not at all	28	12
Not relevant	38	34
	100	100

(continued on next page)

(continued from previous page)

7. "I prefer to be addressed as . . ." [responses of all the women, married plus unmarried]:

Mrs.	44
Miss	13
Ms.	43
	100

Note from Table 1:

Married	55
Separated or divorced	20
Widowed	2
Single	20
Living with man	3
	100

Table 12

Resentment Faced by Women
Figures Are in Percent

1. "Some women have received promotions which otherwise would have gone to men. To what degree do the men resent this? My guess:"

	Female Respondents	Male Respondents
Not at all	9	10
A little	26	38
Somewhat	37	36
A lot	28	16
	100	100

2. Women surveyed: "To a significant degree, I am looked upon by men in my peer group as (may be multiple answers) . . ." Men surveyed: "It is my feeling that a woman in the company who earns $25,000 or more annually is often likely to be looked upon by the men in her peer group as (may be multiple answers) . . ." In percent of 363 female, 306 male tabulated respondents:

	Female Respondents	Male Respondents
An equal, *but*	41	34
Someone who has to be tolerated	10	7
An unwanted competitor	11	6
Unduly favored because a woman	7	12
An inferior	3	2
An equal	37	52
Someone to be respected for her abilities	60	44

(continued on next page)

(continued from previous page)

3. "My guess re: feelings of men's wives towards career women who work as peers with their husbands . . ."

   A. After-hours or out-of-town meetings which include both husbands and career women are resented:

	Female Respondents	Male Respondents
Little or none	22	33
Somewhat	50	45
A lot	28	22
	100	100

   B. Career women are resented in general:

	Female Respondents	Male Respondents
Little or none	29	61
Somewhat	56	36
A lot	15	3
	100	100

See Tables 19, 20, and 21 for responses to open-ended questions.

Table 13

Discrimination Faced by Women
Figures Are in Percent

1. Women respondents: "I would guess that in my company most career women, compared to men in similar jobs and at similar responsibility levels are paid . . ."

At least as well as most men	42
Not as well as most men	58
	100

2. "My feeling about the present likelihood of a woman in the firm being promoted, in competition with a man, given equal qualifications and experience, to and within the following brackets . . ."

   A. Jobs paying $20,000–24,999 annually

	Male Respondents	Female Respondents
For women:		
Greater	29	12
About the same	67	67
Less	4	21
	100	100

   B. Jobs paying $25,000–34,999 annually

For women:		
Greater	17	4
About the same	67	51
Less	16	45
	100	100

   C. Jobs paying $35,000 or more annually

For women:		
Greater	13	2
About the same	42	23
Less	45	75
	100	100

See Table 8 on Affirmative Action.
See Table 5 on jobs held by the organization women surveyed.

Table 14

The Married Woman and Her Career
Figures Are in Percent

1. Marital status of women respondents—See profile, Table 1.

2. "My guess re: whether the following likely would create a significant problem for most career women . . ." (responses of all women, married plus unmarried, respondents) . . . and vs. actual situation (responses of married only):

	Yes	No
A. Earnings of woman exceeding husband's would create problem	64	36
For Marrieds—My earnings exceed those of my husband's	60	40
B. Husband's working for the same employer as wife would create problem	71	29
For Marrieds—My husband and I work for the same employer	13	87

3. "The household chores are mostly . . ." (responses of married women)

Mine	27
My husband's	2
Both	66
Neither	5
	100

4. Career, marriage, quality of life, and health: —Responses of married plus formerly married women—

   A. "Career's effect on my marriage . . ."

Hurt	38
Helped	40
Neither hurt nor helped	18
Don't know	4
	100

   B. "Marriage's effect on my career . . ."

Hurt	28
Helped	38
Neither hurt nor helped	31
Don't know	3
	100

(continued from previous page)

C. "Career's effect on quality of my life . . ."

Hurt	10
Helped	84
Neither hurt nor helped	5
Don't know	1
	100

D. "Combination's effect on my health . . ."

Hurt	35
Helped	24
Neither hurt nor helped	31
Don't know	10
	100

5. See Table 4, Item 4 for data on financial considerations, marriage and career.

6. "My opinion as to whether marriage is likely to interfere with, or to improve the ability of a career woman to . . ." (male responses)

	Do her job well	Advance in her career
A. Without children:		
Interfere with	7	10
Improve	32	33
Neither	61	57
	100	100
B. With children:		
Interfere with	55	55
Improve	4	3
Neither	41	42
	100	100

7. See Table 11, Item 1D re: travel, Item 4B re: transfers and Item 5 re: bringing at-work problems into the home—for the opinions of the women surveyed on whether these create significant problems for career women.

See Chapter 10 for difference in responses of married and separated/divorced women.

Table 15

Sex and Sexual Overtones—Advantage or Not?
Figures Are in Percent

"My opinion as to the value of the following to career women in further-ing their advancement . . ."

	Male Respondents	Female Respondents
1. Good looks		
Some advantage	49	58
A little advantage	43	34
No advantage	8	6
Disadvantage	0.3	2
	100	100
2. Being slender		
Some advantage	43	54
A little advantage	44	36
No advantage	13	10
Disadvantage	0	0.3
	100	100
3. Dressing: Sexy most of the time		
Some advantage	1	2
A little advantage	5	5
No advantage	20	19
Disadvantage	74	74
	100	100
Sexy occasionally		
Some advantage	4	4
A little advantage	29	23
No advantage	40	34
Disadvantage	27	39
	100	100
Conservatively most of the time		
Some advantage	44	66
A little advantage	42	24
No advantage	13	9
Disadvantage	1	1
	100	100

Casually most of the time
    Some advantage   2   4
    A little advantage   10   10
    No advantage   35   42
    Disadvantage   53   44
                                                  100   100

4. Flirting occasionally
    Some advantage   1   5
    A little advantage   20   28
    No advantage   29   35
    Disadvantage   50   32
                                                  100   100

5. An affair with the boss or other
   influential males
    Some advantage   4   4
    A little advantage   6   3
    No advantage   11   13
    Disadvantage   79   80
                                                  100   100

Table 16

*Sex and Sexual Overtones—Frequency
Figures Are in Percent*

"My guess as to the frequency with which the following occurs in my firm . . ."

	Male Respondents	Female Respondents
1. Flirting by career women		
Never or rarely	44	21
Infrequently but occasionally	55	70
Often	1	9
	100	100
2. Affairs with the boss or other influential males		
Never or rarely	70	53
Infrequently but occasionally	29	44
Often	1	3
	100	100
3. Affairs with non-influential males in the company		
Never or rarely	53	46
Infrequently but occasionally	45	47
Often	2	7
	100	100
4. Sexual harassment of career women		
(A) Actual intimacy		
Never or rarely	83	78
Infrequently but occasionally	16	21
Often	1	1
	100	100
(B) Proposed (at least semi-seriously) intimacy		
Never or rarely	53	47
Infrequently but occasionally	45	46
Often	2	7
	100	100

(C) Touching

Never or rarely	51	41
Infrequently but occasionally	46	46
Often	3	13
	100	100

(D) Verbally other than (B)

Never or rarely	38	35
Infrequently but occasionally	55	47
Often	7	18
	100	100

Table 17

Use of Sexual Connotation or Sex on the Job by Career Women
Figures Are in Percent

	Male Respondents	Female Respondents
1. By the way they dress		
Never or rarely	48	41
Infrequently but occasionally	49	52
Often	3	7
	100	100
2. By appeals to male gallantry/ protectiveness		
Never or rarely	44	30
Infrequently but occasionally	52	60
Often	4	10
	100	100
3. By proposing intimacy (at least semi-seriously)		
Never or rarely	80	68
Infrequently but occasionally	19	30
Often	1	2
	100	100
4. By actual intimacy (women seek/encourage)		
Never or rarely	87	70
Infrequently but occasionally	13	28
Often	0.3	2
	100	100
5. By verbal innuendo or repartee other than 3.		
Never or rarely	54	43
Infrequently but occasionally	43	49
Often	3	8
	100	100

Table 18

Factors for Getting Ahead

"What I consider to be the most important factor(s) in addition to job performance, for a woman's getting ahead in my company:"

Male Respondents—Percent of 306 tabulated returns mentioning an item in each category. Some returns gave no, some one, and some multiple responses.

	Percent
"Fitting in," "people" skills	23
Qualifications, experience, and upgrading thereof	21
Self-confidence, drive, hard work, willingness to accept responsibility, dependability	20
Professional attitudes	12
Managerial outlook and temperament	12
Other categories	16

Female Respondents—Percent of 363 tabulated returns mentioning an item in each category. Some returns gave no, some one, and some multiple responses.

Self-confidence, drive, hard work, willingness to accept responsibility, dependability	31
"Fitting in," "people" skills	26
Qualifications, experience, and upgrading thereof	26
Political savvy	12
Professional attitudes	11
Opportunity	9
Managerial outlook and temperament	7
Mentor	6
Other categories	8

Table 19

Obstacles to Getting Ahead

"What I consider to be the greatest obstacle(s) to a woman's getting ahead in my company . . ."

Male Responses—Percent of 306 tabulated returns which include an opinion in the indicated category. Some returns gave no, some one, and some multiple responses.

	Percent
Male chauvinism	27
Lack of qualifications—education/training and experience	13
Lack of professional attitudes	10
Lack of self-confidence, assertiveness, drive and commitment (hard work/long hours); and interference from needs of family	15
Expectations of preferred treatment for women, oversensitivity to supposed discrimination; difficulties in relating to and getting the support of other women, playing on sex	7
There are no obstacles	8
All other	11

Female Responses—Percent of 363 tabulated returns which include an opinion in the indicated category. Some returns gave no, some one, and some multiple responses.

Male chauvinism	53
Lack of qualifications—education/training and experience	17
Attitudes	5
Lack of dedication	5
Lack of self-confidence, assertiveness	3
There are no obstacles	5
Other	7

Table 20

Men's Difficulties Working with Women

Male Respondents: "What I consider to be the most difficult, irritating, frustrating, and/or distasteful problem(s) in working with career women . . ."—percent of 306 tabulated returns mentioning an item in each category. (Some multiple responses.)

Emotionalism	9	
Sensitivity to criticism, personalization of issues/ decisions/conflicts	5	14
Oversensitivity to discrimination, overplaying liberation		5
Expecting undue preferences because of being a woman	5	7
Using or trying to use sex for advantage	2	
Overcomplaining, bitchiness, pettiness		3
Unprofessional attitudes		2
Women's resentment of, competitiveness with, and lack of support for other women		2
Overly aggressive, assertive, arrogant	8	10
Trying to act like a man (rough language, etc.)	2	
Indecisiveness	5	
Lack of flexibility	3	10
Tunnel vision	2	
Priority of family considerations interfering with priority of company needs		6
Other		7
None other than what applies to men		21

Table 21

Women's Difficulties Working with Men and Women

Female Respondents: "What I consider to be the most difficult, irritating, frustrating and/or distasteful problem(s) for me as a woman working with . . ."—percent of 363 tabulated returns mentioning an item in each category. (Some multiple responses.)

With Men

Male chauvinism/condescension	51
Harassment	13
Unequal treatment (working harder/longer with less pay/promotion)	9
Inferior male performance	7
Other	9
No problems	6

With other women:

Their resentment, lack of support, competitiveness, distrust	33
Gossip, pettiness, emotionalism, overcomplaining, over-reacting	18
Self-denigration, indecisiveness, unprofessional attitudes, defensiveness, overbearing, expectation of preference without adequately working for it	20
Other	11
No problems	7

References

1. *U.S. News & World Report,* Mar. 22, 1982, p. 77.
2. Kanter, R. M. *Men and women of the corporation.* New York, NY: Basic Books, Inc., 1977, p. 41.
3. LaRouche, J., and Ryan, R. *Strategies for women at work.* New York, NY: Avon Books, 1984, pp. 181, 182.
4. *The Wall Street Journal,* Nov. 2, 1982, p. 29.
5. *Statistical abstracts of the United States—1984,* pp. 169, 170.
6. *U.S. News & World Report,* Feb. 8, 1982, p. 63.
7. *The Wall Street Journal,* June 16, 1981.
8. *Business Week,* June 28, 1982, p. 10.
9. Hennig, M., and Jardim, A. *The managerial woman.* New York, NY: Pocket Books, 1978, p. 140.
10. Kanter, R. M. *Men and women of the corporation.* New York, NY: Basic Books, Inc., 1977, p. 107.
11. *The Wall Street Journal,* April 14, 1981.
12. Zey, M. G. *The mentor connection.* New York, NY: Dow Jones-Irwin, 1984, p. 114.
13. *Statistical abstracts of the United States—1984,* pp. 419, 420.
14. Cox, A. *The Cox report on the American corporation.* New York, NY: Delacorte Press, 1982, p. 284.
15. Kanter, R. M. *Men and women of the corporation.* New York, NY: Basic Books, Inc., 1977, pp. 58, 59.
16. Kanter, R. M. *Men and women of the corporation.* New York, NY: Basic Books, Inc., 1977, pp. 197 ff.
17. Zey, M. G. *The mentor connection.* New York, NY: Dow Jones-Irwin, 1984, p. 117.
18. Zey, M. G. *The mentor connection.* New York, NY: Dow Jones-Irwin, 1984, pp. 126 ff.
19. Easton, S., Mills, J. M., and Winokur, D. K. *Equal to the task: How working women are managing in corporate America.* New York, NY: Putnam Publishing Group, 1982, p. 120.
20. Collins, E. G. C., and Blodgett, T. *Harvard Business Review,* March-April 1981, pp. 76 ff.

Bibliography

Appelbaum, E. *Back to work: Determinants of women's successful re-entry.* Boston, MA: Auburn House Publishing Co., 1981.

Bernardin, J.H. *Women in the work force.* New York, NY: Praeger Publishers, 1982.

Blaxall, M. (Ed.). *Women & the workplace: Implications of occupational segregation.* Chicago, IL: University of Chicago Press, 1976.

Burrow, M.G. *Developing women managers: What needs to be done?* New York, NY: American Management Associations, 1978.

Cannie, J.K. *The woman's guide to management success: How to win power in the real organizational world.* Englewood Cliffs, NJ: Prentice-Hall, Inc., 1979.

Carr-Ruffino, N. *The promotable woman.* Belmont, CA: Wadsworth Publishing, 1982.

Douglass, D.N. *Choice seven compromise: A woman's guide to balancing family & career.* New York, NY: American Management Associations, 1983.

Easton, S., Mills, J.M., & Winokur, D.K. *Equal to the task: How working women are managing in corporate America.* New York, NY: Putnam Publishing Group, 1982.

Farley, J. *Affirmative action & the woman worker: Guidelines for personnel management.* New York, NY: American Management Associations, 1979.

Fenn, M. *Making it in management: A behavioral approach for women executives.* Englewood Cliffs, NJ: Prentice-Hall, Inc., 1978.

Fox, M.F. *Women at work.* Palo Alto, CA: Mayfield Publishing Co., 1983.

Foxworth, J. *Boss lady.* New York, NY: Warner Books, Inc., 1979.

Frank, H.H. *Women in the organization.* Philadelphia, PA: University of Pennsylvania Press, 1977.

French, L., & Stewart, D. *Women in business.* Milwaukee, WI: Raintree Publishers, Inc., 1979.

Halcomb, R. *Women making it.* New York, NY: Ballantine Books, Inc., 1979.

Hennig, M., & Jardim, A. *The managerial woman.* New York, NY: Doubleday & Co., Inc., 1978.

Higginson, M.V., & Quick, T.L. *The ambitious woman's guide to a successful career.* New York, NY: American Management Associations, 1980.

Josefowitz, N. *Paths to power: A woman's guide from first job to top executive.* New York, NY: Addison House, 1980.

Kanter, R.M. *Men and women of the corporation.* New York, NY: Basic Books, Inc., 1977.

Kleinman, C. *Women's networks.* New York, NY: Ballantine Books, Inc., 1981.

LaRouche, J., & Ryan, R. *Strategies for women at work.* New York, NY: Avon Books, 1984.

Lee, N. *Targeting the top.* New York, NY: Doubleday & Co., Inc., 1980.

Loring, R., & Wells, T. *Breakthrough: Women into management.* New York, NY: Van Nostrand—Reinhold Co., 1972.

Lynch, E.M. *The woman's guide to management.* New York, NY: Cornerstone Library, Inc., 1978.

McLane, H.J. *Selecting, developing and retaining women executives: A corporate strategy for the eighties.* New York, NY: Van Nostrand Reinhold Co., Inc., 1980.

Newton, D.A. *Think like a man, act like a lady, work like a dog.* New York, NY: Doubleday & Co., Inc., 1979.

Nieva, V. & Gutek, B. *Women & work: A psychological perspective.* New York, NY: Doubleday & Co., Inc., 1981.

Pinkstaff, M.A. & Wilkinson, A.B. *Women at Work: Overcoming the Obstacles.* New York, NY: A & W Publishers, Inc., 1979.

Thompson, A.M., & Wood, M.D. *Management strategies for women.* New York, NY: Simon & Schuster, 1980.

Trahey, J. *Jane Trahey on women and power.* New York, NY: Rawson Associates Publishers, Inc., 1977.

Wallace, P.A. *Women in the workplace.* Boston, MA: Auburn House Publishing Co., 1982.

Wallach, A.T. *Women's work.* New York, NY: New American Library, Inc., 1981.

Walshok, M.L. *Blue collar women.* New York, NY: Doubleday & Co., Inc., 1981.

Ward, P.A., & Stout, M.G. *Women at Work.* Grand Rapids, MI: Zondervan Corp., 1981.

Welch, M. *Networking.* New York, NY: Harcourt Brace Jovanovich, Inc., 1980.

Zey, M.G. *The mentor connection.* New York, NY: Dow Jones—Irwin, 1984.

Zimmerman, J. (Ed.). *The technological woman: Interfacing with tomorrow.* New York, NY: Praeger Publishers, 1983.

Index

Absenteeism, 118
Advertising, 11, 85
Affirmative action, 55, 57–58, 75,
    81, 86, 89, 144, 176
Age, 148
Age Discrimination and
    Employment Act, 148
Aggressiveness, 21–22, 24, 30, 56,
    195
  as managerial trait, 35–44
Arrogance, 42–43, 195
Assertiveness, 36, 40, 41, 42, 46,
    194
  see also Aggressiveness

Banking, 11, 21, 45
Bonuses, 76
Bosses, 37–38, 82
  communication with, 46
  evaluating, 92
  female, 59, 70–73, 75, 78–80,
    133–134
  loyalty to, 51
  male, 20, 23, 31–32, 33, 45, 71,
    86–87, 130
  and male chauvinism, 60–61, 69
  as mentors, 49–50, 87
  in politics, 50

and promotion, 86–87
and risk-taking, 99–104
understanding, 96–99, 111
Budgets, 109–110

Career vs. marriage, 12, 114, 186
  and children, 114, 116, 117,
    118–120, 121, 126
  and health, 122, 123, 124
  and relocation, 120–121
Children, 114, 116, 117, 118–120,
    121, 123, 126
Civil Rights Act of 1964, 141
Commission system, 76
Communication, 44–45, 77
Comparable worth, 146
Competition, 54–57, 58, 59–60, 77
Costs, cutting, 97–99, 110
Criticism, sensitivity to, 25, 82,
    195
Cultural conditioning, 29

Decision making, 23, 25, 28–30,
    46, 125
Delegating, 47, 78–80, 82
Discrimination, 58, 60, 62, 64, 68,
    82, 89, 117, 141–149, 185

age, 148
class actions in, 143–144
as disparate treatment, 143, 144
in physical requirements,
    142–143
in pregnancy, 145
Divorce, 113, 116
Dress, 22, 58, 128–129, 188

Emotionalism, 23–24, 26, 82, 195,
    196
Employment agencies, 86, 141, 175
Equal Employment Opportunity
    Commission (EEOC), 141,
    146
Equal Pay Act of 1963 (EPA),
    145, 146
Equal to the Task (Eastman,
    Mills, & Winokur), 97
Equality, 55–56
of opportunity, 15, 142
Exclusion, 66–67
Exposure, 83–84

Firing, 26, 28, 75
unfair, 148–149
Fringe benefits, 76

Goals
individual, 48
management, 108

Hennig, Margaret, 57
High technology, 11, 32
Humor, sense of, 23

Image, 48–49
physical, 128, 188
Impermanence, 121–122, 139–140,
    171
Intelligence, 21

Jardim, Anne, 57
Job changing, 85, 94–95, 140, 177
Job classifications, 15–16, 63
Jobs, starting, 174

Kanter, Rosabeth M., 22, 58, 66,
    71

LaRouche, Janice, 24
Lay-offs; *see* Firing
Line management, 28, 32, 46, 82,
    94, 106–107
Loyalty, 22, 51, 106

Male chauvinism, 12, 16, 43,
    60–64, 66, 69, 71, 81, 82, 117,
    194, 196
Management
authoritarian, 73–74
levels of, 32, 33
by objective, 107–108
participative, 73–74
styles of, 73–75
traits, 35–53
types of, 28
Managerial Woman, The (Hennig
    & Jardim), 57
Marketing, opportunities in, 85

rriage, 123-126
ee also Career vs. marriage;
  Spouses
ntor Connection, The (Zey), 62,
  68
ntors, 16, 46, 49, 50, 87-88,
  102, 193
rale, 74, 76, 80
tivation, 45
f subordinates, 75-80

otiation, 38
works, 46, 49, 50, 88
ton, Derek A., 21

ectivity, 23, 24
ortunities, 83-90
quality of, 15, 142
aluating present, 92-93
anization (quality of), 30-31
anization chart, 105

creases, 39, 75-76
equality of, 9, 64, 125,
  145-146
ales, 75, 173
ning, 111-112
ics, 48-53, 68, 82
ticality, 31-34
nancy Discrimination Act of
  1978, 145
sure, working under, 26, 82
essionalism, 22, 23, 82, 193,
  194
notion, 12, 38-41, 47, 84, 86,
  175, 176

and affirmative action, 57-58
and arrogance, 44
inequalities in, 64, 185
as motivation, 76
and new responsibilities, 42
opportunities for, 84
politics in, 48-50
and relocation, 121, 124
stress of, 26
Public relations, 11, 85

Questionnaires
  for men, 160-165
  for women, 152-159
  see also Surveys
Quotas; *see* Affirmative action

Recruiters, 86, 175
Referrals, 86, 175
Relocation, 42, 81-82, 83,
  120-121, 125, 138-139,
  181-182
Resentment
  by male peers, 54-56, 57, 71,
    75, 130, 183
  by spouses, 58, 68, 184
  by subordinates, 128, 130
  by women, 59, 71-73, 128, 133,
    195, 196
Responsibility, taking, 42, 83, 193
Risk-taking, 45-47, 99-104
Role models, 9
Ryan, Regina, 24

Salaries; *see* Pay
Schwimmer, Lawrence D., 35

Secretarial work, 16, 17, 41,
    61–63, 85
Self-confidence, 27, 46, 193, 194
Seniority systems, 145
Sexual aspects, 12, 22, 58, 82, 88,
    124, 126, 127–137, 138,
    188–192
  harassment, 22, 66, 82, 131–133,
    135, 190, 196
    and EEOC, 146–148
  office affairs, 133–135, 189, 190
Silberg, Carol, 22
Skills, special, 83
Socializing, 67–68, 126, 133, 138,
    179–181
Spouses, 58–59, 82, 88, 116,
    117–118, 124–125, 134
Staff positions, 28, 32, 46, 82, 94,
    106–107
Status symbols, 76
Stress, job, 26, 124, 178
Subordinates, 70–80, 82, 170
  and delegating, 47, 78–80
  female, 71–73, 75
    and resentment, 128, 130

  male, 70–71, 75
  monitoring of, 78–79
  motivation of, 75
  spouses of, 59
Surveys
  parameters, 18–19, 150–151
  respondents, 166–167, 172
  responses, 19, 166–196
  see also Questionnaires

*Think Like a Man, Act Like a
    Lady, Work Like a Dog*
    (Newton), 21
Title, job, 76, 93, 105–106
Title VII (Civil Rights Act of
    1964), 141, 143, 145, 146
Transfers; *see* Relocation
Travel, 76, 118, 120, 123–124,
    125, 126, 138, 179

Working harder (women), 20–21

Zey, Michael G., 62, 88